# **A**ttitudes **S**kills **K**nowledge:

## how to teach learning-to-learn in the secondary school

MEETING THE CHALLENGES OF TWENTY-FIRST CENTURY LEARNING

**JULIET STRANG**
**PHILIP MASTERSON**
**OLIVER BUTTON**

**Edited by Bill Lucas**

Crown House Publishing Limited
www.crownhouse.co.uk

Published by
Crown House Publishing Ltd
Crown Buildings, Bancyfelin, Carmarthen, Wales, SA33 5ND, UK
www.crownhouse.co.uk
and
Crown House Publishing Company LLC
6 Trowbridge Drive, Suite 5, Bethel, CT 06801-2858, USA
www.CHPUS.com

© Juliet Strang, Philip Masterson, Oliver Button 2006

British Library of Cataloguing-in-Publication Data
A catalogue entry for this book is available from the British Library.

**International Standard Book Number**
1-845-90024-3
978-1-845-90024-3

**Library of Congress Control Number**
2006932143

Editor: Bill Lucas
Project management: Janice Baiton Editorial Services, Cambridge
Design and typesetting: Paul Barrett Book Production, Cambridge
Illustrations: Les Evans
Printed and bound in the UK by Cromwell Press, Trowbridge, Wiltshire

# Contents

# Foreword

Learning-to-learn is, in my view, UK education's top priority. Everyone is talking about it. Learning-to-learn is the most fundamental aspect of personalised learning; it goes to the heart of the primary–secondary transition agenda; top trainers such as Bill Lucas, Alistair Smith, Guy Claxton and Ian Gilbert are on a mission to promote it; tutors in further and higher education want students to be more independent; and employers are looking for high levels of initiative, teamwork and self-sufficiency. Changing patterns in society and the economy are requiring people to be even more adaptable and inventive. Thinking skills are in the air and creativity is high on the national agenda.

*Attitudes Skills Knowledge: how to teach learning-to-learn in the secondary school* is appearing at just the right moment. Many secondary schools tell me that results have reached a plateau and they are now looking to promote generic skills as a way of securing higher levels of attainment and achievement. In England, the Qualifications and Curriculum Authority is reviewing the Key Stage 3 curriculum with a view to reducing prescription and increasing both flexibility and continuity, and, in Wales, the Department for Education, Lifelong Learning and Skills is pursuing a skills-based ethos at Key Stage 4. These official moves create the ideal 'permitting circumstances' for innovative learning-to-learn developments.

People are realising that the world is changing and that new skills are required. There is, without doubt, a growing consensus about the importance of students acquiring an understanding of the learning process and becoming skilled in, and disposed towards, autonomous, lifelong learning. In response, many schools have introduced a learning-to-learn course of some kind – either as a timetabled subject in its own right, or as a major feature of personal, social and health education. Others hope that special 'learning days', often led by specialist agencies, will deliver the goods. Villiers High School has gone further and developed a framework for teaching all-important generic learning skills and attitudes through ordinary lessons across the whole curriculum. This is both exciting and ambitious.

My own work over the years has led me to believe that the outcomes we now want for students – a set of effective learning habits, deep personal awareness, a repertoire of technical learning skills and an internalised acceptance of personal and social responsibility – cannot be achieved through small-scale interventions. These qualities and abilities can only be developed over a long period of time, through consistent work in multiple contexts. A successful learning-to-learn initiative, therefore, has to start in Year 7 and has to feature regularly and prominently in students' school-wide experiences. It means, in practice, asking teachers to design particular sorts of lessons, to pose particular sorts of questions and to behave in particular sorts of ways; it requires them to debrief learning with students, which in turn requires them to have a grasp of the whole learning-to-learn agenda – no matter what subject they teach. Fundamentally, it boils down to asking all teachers to become enthusiastic advocates of the learning process, not just teachers of their specific subjects. For many, this involves a significant change in persona and style.

Over recent years, Villiers High School has worked hard to achieve just this. Like most London schools, it faces considerable challenges: a diverse student population with many different backgrounds and languages, and, in many cases, with relatively low levels of English; a steady turnover of staff; many students with limited life experience and no academic tradition within their families; and a significant number of teachers who are transient and who do not have an immediate grasp of the context and current needs of UK education. Consequently, the learning-to-learn programme has had to 'cook slowly'. In fact, it has taken three years to define and refine the framework of skills and attitudes, to win the hearts and minds of staff and to deliver sufficient training and coaching. Prior to this, a further four years were spent ploughing the ground – working with colleagues on issues such as kinaesthetic learning, constructivism, group-work, peer teaching, differentiation, assessment, peer lesson observation and personal development planning. Curriculum leaders, pastoral leaders, classroom teachers and learning assistants were all expected to review and develop their practice regularly. This long learning journey has required the strong, visionary and consistent leadership of senior staff, a point that needs to be underlined: significant whole-school change of the learning-to-learn kind, which involves a redefinition of a school's priorities and purpose, can only be achieved with conviction at the top.

Having said all this, there is still a great deal to do in order to embed the learning-to-learn programme deeply enough for it to be self-sustaining. Villiers is not immune from all the usual school emergencies that absorb unreasonable amounts of time and energy or from all the mundane pressures that subtly pull people back towards ordinary practice and ordinary priorities. This book, therefore, is realistic. It is full of down-to-earth pragmatism and hard-won wisdom. There is nothing superficial or unworkable here.

What you get is a treasure trove of material. You can use this book as a short cut for your thinking. A full learning-to-learn programme is unfolded for you with advice on how to implement it. This book contains initial lesson plans; practical strategies for more advanced classroom work; tips and pointers for further development; ladders of learning-to-learn progression that enable you to track students' growth in key areas; ideas for exciting out-of-class initiatives such as student conferences and student lesson observers; a rationale that will help you to convince your colleagues; and a survey of leadership issues and implications.

Over the last eight years, it has been my genuine pleasure to work with these educators, many of whom are now my friends. I heartily commend this book to you. It is the real work of real teachers in a real school. They have forged an approach to the nation's most pressing education issue that translates the theory and rhetoric into classroom action. You can adopt their template or customise it; you can read this book as a stimulating case study or as a blueprint. Either way, it will enrich your thinking and practice, and ultimately bring great benefits to your students.

Paul Ginnis
July 2006

# Preface

*Attitudes Skills Knowledge: how to teach learning-to-learn in the secondary school* is about the learning-to-learn approaches that Villiers High School have been pioneering since 2003.

Villiers is a mixed 11–16 community comprehensive school in Southall. There are 1200 students on roll, with 98 per cent from ethnic minority backgrounds. The number of students taking free school meals is well above average and student population shows relatively high levels of social deprivation (1316 out of 8414). There is significant mobility with many students joining the school throughout the year.

Overall, the school is successful and this is the result of the hard work and expertise of its staff. While Villiers' performance is average compared to national norms, it is good when compared to similar schools. The value added from Key Stage 2 to Key Stage 4 is high. However, I am constantly looking for ways in which we can improve.

The learning-to-learn curriculum was born out of the desire to increase the effectiveness of what we do as a school. When I arrived at Villiers as headteacher in January 1997, the staff and I started to work very deliberately on developing our teaching and learning expertise. At about this time, I met Paul Ginnis at a conference hosted by the Centre for the Study of Comprehensive Schools. Over the past eight years, the staff at Villiers have been lucky to have worked with Paul and also a number of leading thinkers, including Guy Claxton and Bill Lucas.

From the very first occasion I worked with staff to look at our development as a school, the desire to develop students' independent learning abilities came up as a recurrent theme at staff development planning meetings. It was only after a number of attempts to develop such abilities that it became clear that students would not become the independent learners we wanted unless we gave them the skills to do so. At the time we came to this conclusion, I had recently promoted two staff to become advanced skills teachers (ASTs) in addition to the one already in place at the school. It made sense for these ASTs to work on developing the learning-to-learn curriculum. They started with guidance and help from Paul Ginnis.

An initial research phase involving reading and visiting other schools was followed by a period of experimenting with ideas in the classroom, much discussion and the first written drafts of our approach to a learning-to-learn curriculum. Interested teachers were invited to join a 'core' learning-to-learn team and they continued to experiment with ideas in the classroom, building up a bank of lessons to be shared by all staff.

In the middle of this process, we considered different models for implementation of the curriculum; for example, discrete learning-to-learn lessons (rather like study skills in PSHE), having a Year 7 curriculum based on themes and skills taught by a 'special team' of trained teachers, and integrating learning-to-learn into the curriculum.

The decision to integrate learning-to-learn across the curriculum was taken for a variety of reasons. Research shows that learning skills does not take place in a vacuum. There has to be some content to manipulate. The content has to be sufficiently engaging for the students and they have to see it as worthwhile. The experience of study skills programmes showed us that students seem not to transfer skills from these programmes to their subjects. We were worried about having a special team to deliver learning-to-learn. Although this might work in the short term, there would be problems if team members left, the team might be seen as elite and it would not really help to move the whole school forward. A learning-to-learn curriculum that would genuinely move the school forward would need to be accessible to, and taught by, all teachers.

Taking a cross-curricular route for developing learning-to-learn is more challenging but we felt it was worthwhile.

Our learning-to-learn curriculum was launched with all staff at Villiers on two in-service training days in March 2004, prior to its formal debut for Year 7 in September. The training days involved teachers teaching live demonstration lessons to students with the other teachers as the audience (see Chapter 12 for more on this). 'Gained time' in the summer term was used to develop learning-to-learn lessons ready for September.

As a result of staff changes that took place, the development of learning-to-learn was taken over by two assistant headteachers, Phil Masterson and Olly Button, along with AST Amarjit Garcha. We have written this book together. However, the ideas for lessons published here are derived from many teachers working at Villiers and it is this, we hope, that gives Section 2 of this book, which is full of ideas for teachers, its validity and credibility.

Since starting on this journey with learning-to-learn, the notion of 'personalised learning' has come to the fore on the national agenda for educational change and so it is worth highlighting exactly how the Villiers' rationale and approach to introducing an integrated learning-to-learn curriculum dovetails with the national agenda of personalising learning.

> 'It is our responsibility to make the education system fit the needs of all children. We need to unlock everyone's diverse capabilities. This doesn't mean one-to-one tuition, it does mean responding to the individual needs of children who are stuck, bored or demotivated and re-engaging them with the education system.'

> *Alan Johnson*, Secretary of State for Education and Skills, May 2006

Our view of personalising learning at Villiers has been about maximising the learning outcomes of all students by empowering them to take more proactive responsibility for their own learning. Or, put another way, to teach our students to become effective independent learners with a good command of not only *what* needs to be learned and *how* it might best be learned, but also with the right dispositions to learn effectively. Clearly, then, the introduction of a learning-to-learn curriculum is a logical and appropriate way to address the personalising learning agenda.

It is early days for us in evaluating the impact of our work, but thus far the signs are that, on all fronts – observed improved quality of learning in classrooms, external tests, teacher motivation and pupil engagement – the learning-to-learn curriculum is transforming the learning and teaching at our school.

Juliet Strang
Headteacher
July 2006

# Acknowledgements

We would like to thank the following who have all, in different ways, helped:

John Abbot, Nicolas Armet, Pam Ash, Hulya Baillie, Martin Baillie, John Browne, Maria Chughtai, Guy Claxton, Michelle Collings, Paul Craven, Caroline Cuinet, Dave Curran, Francis Duah, Paul Ginnis, Iftikar Gondal, Joel Grant, Amanda Green, Jo Halford, Machel Hewitt, Marie Hinkson, Mumin Humayun, Dai Jones, Deborah Khan, Nusrul Khan, Daniel Kia, Bill Lucas, Kim Ly, Guy Maidment, Victoria Mandhiza, Fran McClelland, Peter McGonigle, Helen McGrath, Aaron McInnis, Matthew Moss School, Gopali Nagi, Michael O'Neil, Sukvinder Sagoo, Amanda Sara, Christine Sheppard, Emma Sims, Lauren Smith, Malcolm Spoor, Daisy Rana, Kai Vacher, Amarjit Virdee and Fabienne Warrington.

And special thanks to our student lesson observers:

Fardowsa Ali, Jason Bhatti, Supreet Dhindsa, Ilhan Farah God, Parampreet Heer, Sandeep Hundal, Ayesha Hussain, Simran Johal, Akash Kamboj, Rebecca Kumar, Rita Majauskite, Gurnoor Nagi, Rahim Nizarali, Sail Premgy, Seema Rehensi, Kirandeep Saroay, Bhavna Sharma, Nandini Soni, Kerri Thomas and Pavithra Yogeswaran.

# PART 1

What we do and
why we do it

# Introduction to Part 1

Part 1 describes the first section of the journey by the staff at Villiers School to discover more about how students learn and how to create a school where opportunities for students to become effective lifelong learners are maximised. The ASK approach is described and some strategies are outlined that we firmly believe go to make up effective learners.

In the remainder of the book, ASK is explained in more detail. Part 2 provides some exemplary materials for teaching ASK. These examples have been devised, tried and tested by teachers at Villiers. Suggestions are supplied for how to apply these 'learning episodes' in different subjects and how students might be expected to make progress in the different areas of ASK.

Part 3 gives illustrations of ASK outside the classroom: our learning-to-learn student conference and our student lesson observers. And, finally, there is a discussion on some aspects of the implementation of learning-to-learn at Villiers in order to give useful ideas and highlight some of the issues for teachers and schools wishing to introduce learning-to-learn.

# 1 About learning-to-learn

*'We should try and turn out people who love learning so much and learn so well that they will be able to learn whatever needs to be learned.'*

JOHN HOLT

## COMING UP IN THIS CHAPTER:

▶ Why learning-to-learn?
▶ What is learning-to-learn?
▶ What approach did we take and why?
▶ The outcomes and benefits of learning-to-learn.
▶ A vision of the future of learning-to-learn.

## Why learning-to-learn?

Teaching has been described as the art of pushing string. In other words, the hard work teachers put in is not always rewarded by the learning outcomes they expect. Juliet describes the following early experience as a trainee teacher:

> 'I had just started out on a PGCE course and had just been teaching a Year 9 group the topic "Microbes". I was travelling home for the weekend and marking their "end of unit" test on the train. The disappointment I felt at the poor quality of their answers obviously showed on my face, as a fellow passenger smiled and said: "Not as easy as you thought, is it?"
>
> At that moment, I realised that up to then my own learning and success had been directly related to the effort and hard work I had put in. But now it was not so simple: getting other people to learn is not at all a straightforward process.'

Has anything like this happened to you?

## What is learning-to-learn?

In a nutshell, learning-to-learn can be described as learning the attitudes, skills and knowledge necessary to become a more effective learner. When learning-to-learn is not built into the curriculum, students may learn these skills by default, by discovering the best ways to learn for themselves. High-attaining students, in particular, often have better developed learning skills than others and arguably this is why they are successful. However, even these students may have some learning skills that are not well developed, relying too much on their ability to memorise large amounts of content. Indeed, one could argue that when employers complain that young people today are not well equipped for the workplace by their education, that they lack the essential skills of communication, teamwork, time management, planning, and problem solving, they are really beginning to talk about what it is to be an effective learner.

## Our approach

Good teachers have always been interested in the process of learning, and insightful educators have written about this process over many decades. But it is only comparatively recently that interest has focused so intensely on the way we learn how to learn and on its likely benefits for students. In the USA, Howard Gardner and David Perkins have transformed our view of intelligence and how it is 'learnable'. And nearer to home, a long list of thinkers and practitioners, including John Abbot, Guy Claxton, Paul Ginnis, Bill Lucas and Alistair Smith, have paved the way for the topic of learning itself to be taken seriously.

A tipping point for us was the launch in the late 1990s by the Campaign for Learning (CfL) of a major national research project into learning-to-learn. Their first report, *Teaching pupils how to learn*, contained a tentative finding – that schools tend to approach learning the wrong way round. They start with **k**nowledge, then develop **s**kills and finally – in rare moments – focus on the **a**ttitudes of students: a 'KSA' approach. Yet what those schools in the CfL project seemed to be doing was to start with the attitudes of lifelong learners – 'ASK'. Like the CfL, we had a strong sense that attitudes were very important, along with the knowledge and skills of learning.

In the early days, we were worried by the fact that many of our students appeared to be unable to tackle learning without being 'spoonfed' by their teachers. They needed a kind of never-ending saline drip of pre-packaged knowledge, making our desire for them to be independent learners a real challenge. But, when we tried to encourage independent learning in lessons and through homework, we found that the majority of students could not do it. They did not know how to organise their time, select resources to use, find out relevant information from text, work together in groups, connect ideas together, plan and so on.

The frustration felt by all of us at Villiers was most acute, and happened every year between October and March when the Year 11 students were in the final stages of preparing for GCSEs. We recognised that by then we were fighting a losing battle. We decided we needed to start in Year 7 and that we needed to teach our students to learn explicitly by including in our curriculum the attitudes, skills and knowledge they would need to become expert learners. The result of all of this at Villiers is that we have developed the 'ASK' approach to learning-to-learn so that it forms the cornerstone of our thinking – our means of helping teachers to help students become effective learners.

The following example illustrates why students need to learn learning attitudes and skills as well as their subject knowledge. It describes how a Year 8 group tackle a task without the help of their teacher. The class have not been taught ASK, but they have had two lessons on how to write for newspapers. The class was observed in order to find out how students tackled the problem, with particular emphasis on assessing group-work skills. The observation formed part of an evaluation of learning-to-learn. This was a year group that had not benefited from learning-to-learn teaching and they were to be compared to the year group that had followed learning-to-learn. These students would be asked to do the same task in the same context when they reached Year 8 and so provide comparative data on group-work skills for those who had and had not been taught ASK.

## Discovering group-work problems

A Year 8 class enters the school library. The class has been divided into groups of four or five students and each group is asked to sit at a table where a task and some resources are ready for the students. The teacher introduces the lesson and sets the task: to produce the front page for *The West London Times*. Specifically, the students are asked to:

- write the headline
- write the first paragraph of the scoop
- decide on a photo to use
- choose which quotations to use from interview sheets provided.

The teacher explains that the students will be working together in groups, but without help from their teachers.

Each group has been given details of a story; key vocabulary; a front page from the previous week and access to interviews with key witnesses. Resources are available for students to help themselves as needed.

Figure 1.1 shows how one group approached the task and other groups were similar.

Students in the group did not communicate with each other about the task at hand. It seemed that they did not have any deliberate strategy to use to work together, to share ideas or to plan their learning. When one girl tried to do this, her attempts were ignored by the others. Furthermore, the group did not seem to have the desire to work together.

How often does this type of situation happen in classrooms across the UK? Have you ever observed anything similar? Perhaps not exactly as in this example, but in a situation where students are asked to work together in groups and they are not able to do so effectively. How much learning time is lost? How many students feel frustrated by a process they cannot engage with?

**5**

**Figure 1.1 Classroom scenario**

When this lesson was discussed with other colleagues who were observers, we suspected that quite a few teachers in our school would not be aware of how limited their students' group-work skills were or how this might be damaging the learning experience. How many teachers get the opportunity to stop and watch what their students do? Would it help you to do this?

It certainly helped our PE staff. At an in-service training day at Villiers, the PE department decided to focus on group-work skills. The head of PE taught a demonstration lesson to a volunteer class. The department watched. He, and the very experienced teachers in the department, admitted to being taken aback by the outcome. Teamwork was the area of the curriculum they prided themselves on. It turned out that, when observed closely, the students did not know how to work effectively in groups. The department had assumed that they did and that they learned group-work through their team games without explicit consideration of group-work skills.

This is why Villiers has developed a learning-to-learn curriculum. We have realised that we cannot expect our students to develop learning skills through osmosis. The classroom time used to teach ASK is well spent because otherwise we end up with the paucity of learning experience described in Figure 1.1 and the fallout from that for students feelings about school, about learning and about the subjects they study.

There is one further point to make about this example. When we observed the lesson and the students' responses, we realised that effective group-work in this case could not be separated from effective planning. Part of the difficulty for students seemed to arise from the lack of planning skills. This illustrates a tension that runs throughout the learning-to-learn curriculum.

We have to separate the learning-to-learn attitudes, skills and knowledge in order to understand them and to teach them to students; however, it must not be forgotten that they all link together in quite involved ways.

## What is the ASK curriculum?

The ASK curriculum is a detailed map of learning-to-learn at Villers, which consists of seven strands of learning-to-learn knowledge and skills and five attitudes integral to these (see Figure 1.2). ASK started from a blank sheet of paper and the first draft was devised by three advanced skills teachers working at Villiers with Paul Ginnis. The final version has been reached through a process of experimenting in many classrooms at Villiers and much drafting and redrafting.

Bransford et al. (2000) describe an experiment carried out by Ericsson et al. in which a college student was given strings of digits to memorise. The experiment took place over 40 days and as it progressed the student was able to memorise an increasing amount of numbers – from an initial seven to over 70 (see Figure 1.3). It seemed that the student did this by developing a mental muscle for memory. However, after the number experiment, when the student was asked to remember strings of letters, he went back to remembering only seven. During the experiment, the student had developed a technique for remembering the number strings: he chunked the numbers into meaningful numbers that he could remember by using the winning times for track races, of which he had extensive knowledge. Thus, he did not develop a memory muscle but rather a technique for memorising.

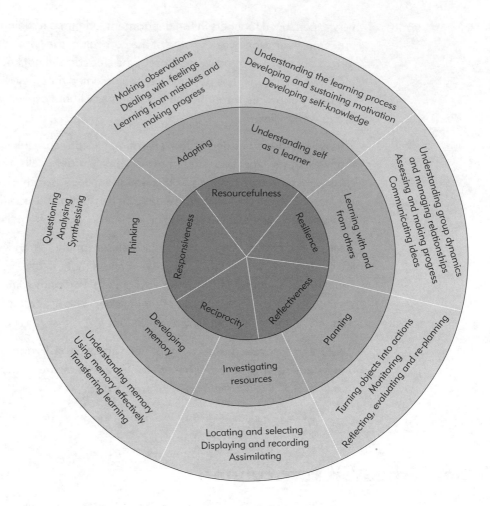

**Figure 1.2  ASK summary**

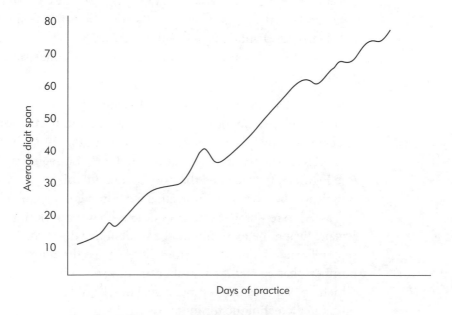

**Figure 1.3  Graph adapted from Bransford et al. (2000)**

In ASK, we set out to teach the students techniques such as chunking and linking memories, at the same time as they learn subject knowledge. By using this method, students can be very deliberate in the way they approach their learning and we help them to do this rather than expecting them to discover it on their own.

The Villiers' approach is to integrate learning-to-learn into all subjects across the school. The experience of teaching discrete study skills programmes convinced us that students need to learn learning skills through specific subject content, so that they have meaning and relevance. However, we knew it would be very important for the learning skills to be taught explicitly, so that students would be aware that they were learning a particular approach or technique and that they would be able to talk about it, analyse it, improve it and choose to use it again. So a very important part of the ASK lessons is the meta-learning element. This is when students and teacher reflect together on how they have been learning and what learning-to-learn skills, knowledge and attitudes they have been developing. It is the time when the student and teacher take a good look at the learning process to see inside the black box of the mind, to unravel the mystery of learning and to share their secrets with each other.

Initially, Villiers introduced ASK to all Year 7 classes in every subject in the curriculum. To begin with, students had a minimum of one ASK lesson every fortnight. Since then, ASK has been extended to Years 8 and 9. At Villiers, the staff are not just teachers of history or science or maths or English, they are all teachers of learning.

## ASK in action – teaching history to Year 7

*A young history teacher describes how he incorporated the skill of connecting ideas into his lessons.*

The learning-to-learn curriculum is something new to me and I decided that I wanted to try out lessons on connecting ideas and information because I thought it would fit in with what we were teaching at the time: 'Why did William win the Battle of Hastings?'

With this topic there are various key factors that need to be identified in order to answer an essay question later. I realised from my teaching practice last year that students found it very hard to connect ideas together to identify such key factors. One key factor would be that William was lucky and there are various pieces of evidence that fall under that category. Students seem to have difficulty working out what evidence goes with what category. So this is where I decided that connecting ideas fitted in.

I thought I could take two approaches – either just tell the pupils about connecting ideas and then get them to do it with information about the Battle of Hastings, or teach them a lesson about connecting ideas first as a concept on its own and then apply it to a history-specific lesson. I decided to develop a learning-to-learn lesson on connecting ideas and teach this first.

I came up with two main activities for the first lesson. The first activity was to give the students single words – for example, plane, car, boat, bicycle and other methods of transport, a cat, a bolt and so on – and simply ask them to group them. Connect them. The majority of students in the class did this in the obvious way: methods of transport, animals and so on. We had a brief discussion about how they grouped the words and the general feedback was: 'Obviously, sir, we look for similarities and we look for differences.'

After that we moved on to the next exercise. In this one they were given sentences on cards and asked to answer the question: 'Why am I the best teacher?'

Off they went and after about six or seven minutes they came up with different groupings for the sentences such as personality, what the lessons are like. I asked them how they worked out the categories and one group said we had to infer the meaning. This surprised me as we had not considered inference yet in history lessons, so I put inference on the board and we talked about what it meant. Then another group said: 'We didn't do it like that, we looked at the words and all the sentences and worked out that those that began with 'He is…' were about you and we looked for keywords in all the sentences, what words meant the same thing.' Which is a kind of inference.

We finished the lesson by summarising the fact that to connect ideas you need to:

■ look for similarities and differences
■ infer meaning
■ look out for keywords or things that mean the same thing.

In the next lesson, I told the class: 'We need to answer the question, "Why did William win the Battle of Hastings?"'

I gave each group in the class an envelope with 12 pieces of evidence and asked them to sort them into categories. They had been learning about the Battle of Hastings but they had not connected the evidence to explain why William won the battle. We started the lesson by reminding ourselves how to connect ideas.

Because I taught this topic in two other schools as a trainee the previous year, I had something to compare it with and it was obvious to me that this time the students had a much better understanding and were able to say which bit of evidence went with what reason for winning. I knew they found it easier to understand because they were actually saying things such as, 'Well, this can't go with this. If you look at it, this is what it means – how could they go together?'

They were actually using the ideas from the previous learning-to-learn lesson. I knew it had had some impact on them. They were able to understand how to go about applying those skills in a history context.

I have a Year 10 group with very able students. They had to write an essay and I presumed that they would be able to categorise the evidence for the essay they were writing, but, when I told them to do this, they did not know what to do. They are high achieving so eventually they got it but they were asking for a lot of help. So I see why learning-to-learn is so important.

In the lesson described on the previous page, you can see how the teacher is integrating the learning-to-learn skill of connecting ideas and information into his history lesson. He decides initially to spend one lesson teaching the skill of connecting ideas and information before the students apply it to help them understand their history topic: 'Why did William win the Battle of Hastings?' This is just one approach that teachers at Villiers have used to integrate ASK across the curriculum.

Sometimes teachers take part of a lesson to teach a skill and go on to develop it within a subject-specific context and sometimes the skill can be worked on over several lessons. You will notice from the account given that the teacher stops to talk about the skill of connecting ideas at regular intervals throughout the lesson so that the students and teacher take the time to, as it were, hold up the skill to the light and examine it. This ensures that they understand it and can use it when they need to. This critical examination of learning processes is what we refer to throughout the book as 'meta-learning'. In Chapter 3 and Part 2, there are examples of strategies that teachers can use to do this with their classes in a variety of ways.

## The outcomes and benefits of learning-to-learn

At the time of writing this book, Villiers is in its third year of developing learning-to-learn and its second year of teaching it. We are not yet in a position to evaluate fully the outcomes of ASK. These will only show up in our quantitative results when the current Year 8 take their SAT exams in 2007. So any evaluation to date can only be reported in qualitative terms – from what the students and teachers say and what we observe of our students in the school.

In broad terms, we envisage that at the end of Key Stage 3 more of our students will be able to think for themselves, to question, to enquire, to evaluate, to collaborate, to research, to be independent of their teachers, and to make more informed choices (about their learning) for themselves. All of this put together will result in students who are more mature and more in control of their learning. Teachers and students will feel they are learning in partnership with each other. We are already seeing this at Villiers with our students taking a greater proactive part in their own learning and in what happens at school.

If the implementation of learning-to-learn is successful then by the time students reach Year 9 they should have high levels of expertise in many areas of ASK. We anticipate a scenario something like the following:

*A teacher introduces a topic and with the class is able to plan the relevant aims and objectives for that topic and how these would be met, what activities would be effective and whether students should study alone or in groups, based on the purpose of the task and the learning outcomes.*

*Having completed the task, the students would naturally review their progress and the targets they had set themselves, evaluate the effectiveness of the learning process they had chosen and make realistic new targets for their learning in the future.*

In other words, the students would be fully engaged in their learning in partnership with their teacher. They would have the vocabulary, skills and knowledge to discuss their learning with their teacher and each other and the attitudes to be able to connect fully with their learning.

# 2 The ASK curriculum

*'I can't do this, sir.'*
*'But I taught it to you last lesson?'*
*'You might have taught it, sir, but that doesn't mean I know it!'*

## COMING UP IN THIS CHAPTER:

▶ The 5Rs – essential attitudes for effective learners.
▶ The seven areas of skill and knowledge for effective learners.

The dialogue above is fictitious. But it is probably a realistic unspoken conversation between a lot of teachers and their students. We have to face the fact that students are not going to learn how to learn better through osmosis.

It makes sense that, in order to be effective learners, students need to develop the right attitudes. To do this, they need to be taught theory and knowledge about learning and how people learn by their subject teachers. They need to be given opportunities to master their learning skills in their subject lessons. In short, there needs to be a learning-centred curriculum that works hand in hand with traditional subject curricula.

Our learning-to-learn curriculum asks the teacher to be a guide, adviser and instructor of learning as well as a more traditional professor of a subject. Teachers are no longer just subject teachers; they have an additional and explicit role as a learning coach. It does not take a psychic to predict most teachers' initial reactions to such a suggestion. Teachers are busy people and busy for good reason – they are constantly planning, demonstrating, marking and, of course, teaching large amounts of subject content. And that is all well and good, but if our fictitious student at the start of this chapter is telling us any sort of truth – and many of us suspect they are – then it is an awful lot of industry for very little reward, for either teacher or student.

Ensuring that learning-to-learn is explicitly present in lessons and school life is going to mean changes. The learning-to-learn skills and attitudes will have to be planned and delivered and opportunities will have to be fitted in. And, yes, it will take time away from delivering subject content.

But, and it is a huge but, as a result, students will have a greater understanding of, and be more involved in, their learning. They will ultimately be empowered to take more responsibility for their learning and more demands can therefore be made of them. It is the old cliché come true – the greater the time devoted early on to basics, the greater the pay back later.

And the reason it has to be the subject teacher? That has always been clear to us. Models that deliver an explicit learning-to-learn curriculum as an additional separate subject fail to ensure that the skills are transferred into the student's learning of subjects. The establishment of skills and knowledge needs to be explicit, but not isolated from subject content. They must be regularly used in real and relevant learning situations and embedded in the subjects that students study. The only way this can be successfully managed is through the classroom teacher. This model of delivery also makes sure that the classroom teacher manages and leads learning-to-learn, making sure that it is relevant to what the students are doing and that the right skills are covered in the right depth for the right subjects.

We have identified five attitudes and seven areas of skills and knowledge that need to be evident at an established level in the work of any effective learner existing within a larger learning community.

## Attitudes of effective learners

Our ASK curriculum map is underpinned by the five attitudes of Resourcefulness, Reciprocity, Resilience, Responsiveness and Reflectiveness.

Attitudes come first. That is to say that, without sufficiently developed attitudes, a student will find it extremely difficult, if not impossible, to develop the skills and knowledge of ASK and, in so doing, become an effective learner.

The attitudes are more difficult to teach explicitly as they are slightly more subjective and less measurable than the skills and knowledge components. Also, it is easier to argue that these are innate personal attributes that at best are the responsibility of the form tutor or PSHE teacher and at worst remain fixed from birth and hence should be left well alone! However, we believe it is *essential* to overcome this mindset and to develop attitudes if we are to achieve our aim of empowering students with not only the skills and knowledge but also the desire and disposition to become lifelong learners able to thrive in a climate of constant change.

In addition to developing attitudes across all curriculum areas, there are also opportunities to develop them during tutor periods, through assemblies and through enrichment projects such as the learning-to-learn student conferences and whole-school initiatives such as pupil lesson observers. Some of these approaches to attitude development will be discussed in later chapters (specifically, Chapters 13 and 14). However, this chapter will concentrate mainly on the development of students' attitudes through teaching in curriculum subject lessons. The reasons for this mirror those outlined in the first chapter, namely, to add meaning and relevance. Arguably, a stronger rationale for attempting to develop students attitudes in this way is that the attitudes are common themes that run through every subject discipline and that students will benefit from seeing these modelled (and personally interpreted) by as many of their teachers as possible in order to help them do the same.

As we discuss and present practical classroom strategies and sample learning episodes in Part 2, you will see that certain skills and knowledge from ASK will 'look different' according to the curriculum subject context in which they are being taught. This contextual variation is less pronounced when developing students' attitudes so there should be fewer barriers to transferability.

Before exploring each of the attitudes in more depth, it is worth noting at this point that *modelling* of the attitudes, in particular with *the teacher acting as the learner*, is a significant starting point in developing them with any class in any subject area. More details about other techniques and practical suggestions will be presented in Part 2.

## Resourcefulness

A resourceful student will be the one who confidently visits the library and selects the most appropriate books or other resources to help them solve a particular problem or complete a given task. They will be the one who uses the internet to help them research a homework or coursework assignment without considering this to be cheating. They will ask questions of parents, older siblings and even other members of the class or school community, not with the intention of getting the work done for them but with the intention of developing their understanding in an efficient way. They will ask appropriate questions at appropriate times and think laterally as well as vertically. Perhaps most importantly of all, the resourceful student will use creativity, imagination and intuition, linked to previous experience, in order to move forwards. In short, they are the student who rarely gets stuck because, as Jean Piaget put it, they 'know what to do when they don't know what to do'.

With this description in mind, the attitude of resourcefulness could be considered to be a necessary pre-requisite or even an 'umbrella' heading for certain skills, sub-skills and knowledge within ASK, specifically: learning with and from others (sub-skills: organising equipment and resources, learning from models of good practice); processing information and thinking (sub-skill: questioning).

## Picture this...

Frustrated at her students' dependence on her and apparent lack of resourcefulness, a maths teacher decides that she will structure her lesson (about angle facts and properties) so as to develop this particular attitude. She makes this explicit to the students before doing the same with the objectives for their learning in mathematics. As part of the 'starter' phase of the lesson, the students brainstorm what it means to be resourceful. For the main part of the lesson, rather than telling the students what they need to know, she directs them to use the resources table in the back corner of the classroom. On this she has laid out an assortment of textbooks, worksheets, maths dictionaries and two laptop computers with internet access. As the teacher, she makes herself available as a resource that can only be used after all the other resources have been. She limits the number of questions any student can ask to help them think carefully about the best way to use such a precious resource!

. . . . . . . . . . . . . . . . . . . . . . . . . . . . . . . . . . . . . . . . . . . . . . . . . . . . . . . . . . . .

## Reciprocity

Students who have high levels of reciprocity will not only be enthusiastic about the prospect of working in a group but will also have the right skills to do this effectively. They will look upon learning with others not as an opportunity to off-load work on their peers but as a means of achieving more learning success than would have been possible by themselves or alternatively as a more efficient way of completing a given task.

They will have developed intra- and inter-personal skills that allow them to communicate their learning with others, compromise, share ideas and negotiate successful outcomes for the learning of all members of the group. They will observe successful learners in their group and emulate those habits displayed that they feel they could successfully adopt and will also learn positively from those they judge to be less successful in their learning.

As with resourcefulness, this description of a reciprocal learner implies that reciprocity is another headline for the following skills and sub-skills of ASK: learning with and from others; understanding self as a learner (sub-skill: knowing self).

Unlike the other attitudes, reciprocity is necessarily related to inter-personal skills and hence is more likely to be affected by age, maturity, gender, ethnic background, home language and other social factors. However, a student with truly advanced levels of reciprocity would be able to accommodate these differences and possibly even use them to enhance the learning experience for all involved.

## Picture this...

In a bid to develop the reciprocity of his class, an English teacher decides to introduce an extra dimension to his lesson in which students are to work in groups. After a brief discussion of the different 'roles' that could be assigned to individual members of a group, the teacher presents each group (of four or five students) with an A4 envelope in which are badges that each student has to choose at random.

The badge displays the student's role within the group and they are not allowed to operate outside of this. Roles might include 'time-keeper', 'chairperson', 'researcher' and so on.

Such an approach makes each student responsible for their particular role and to an extent dependent on the work of the other group members: they are going to have to use reciprocity if they are to succeed.

. . . . . . . . . . . . . . . . . . . . . . . . . . . . . . . . . . . . . . . . . . . . . . . . . . . . . . . . . . . .

## Resilience

A resilient learner has 'stickability' and uses their clear vision of a successful learning outcome to remind themselves why they are doing a particular task. To be resilient requires self-discipline, which, as most teachers know all too well, does not come naturally to all learners – young and old alike! This self-discipline will allow a resilient learner to summon the concentration and determination to keep trying even when they begin to lose focus or interest. It will also help them to manage distractions.

Following on from our earlier description of a learner with high levels of reciprocity, a resilient student will not rely on others (whether peers or adults) to make their learning easier or to 'do the hard work' for them. This illustrates a certain interaction between the attitudes themselves as well as attitudes and skills.

The skills and sub-skills of ASK that are closely linked with resilience include: understanding self as a learner (motivating self-dealing with stress; knowing self-working within concentration span); adapting (learning from mistakes, managing disappointment) and, perhaps less obviously, developing memory, since this requires willpower and sustained effort to perfect both retention and recall.

## Picture this...

In an attempt to make her students more resilient, a science teacher introduces her own version of Guy Claxton's 'stuck poster'. This involves displaying on the 'learning wall' a list of prompts to help students keep going when previously they would have ground to a halt. Questions include, 'Have you tried breaking the problem down into steps?' and 'Have you tried talking it through with a friend?' among others.

. . . . . . . . . . . . . . . . . . . . . . . . . . . . . . . . . . . . . . . . . . . . . . . . . . . . . . . . . . . .

## Responsiveness

A responsive learner will not repeat errors or ineffective strategies while learning. In order to enable them to respond effectively to new and unfamiliar challenges with their learning, responsive learners must draw on past experiences both positive and negative. For this reason, one could argue that the attitude or disposition of reflectiveness is almost a pre-requisite for the responsive learner. However, reflection on the highs and lows of prior learning experiences is not on its own sufficient for responsiveness: having reflected, the learner must evaluate their own performance in order to respond in a truly effective way to a similar but unfamiliar learning challenge.

The ASK skill of adapting is designed to explore and develop the attitude of responsiveness: specifically, the sub-skill learning from mistakes: analyse mistakes and amend future actions accordingly. However, as we saw earlier, the other attitudes are also inextricably linked to this one.

# Picture this…

A geography teacher was becoming increasingly concerned that his students' focus on receiving assessment feedback was to measure how well they had performed relative to their friends and the rest of the class but with little thought as to how they might improve in the future. To remedy this and to make his students more responsive, he directed the students to identify just one aspect of their work that they would commit to improving the next time they undertook a similar task. He recorded these in his record book and made the students aware that this would be the first aspect of their next piece of work that he would assess.

## Reflectiveness

We have already seen that reflectiveness is necessary in order for a learner to be responsive and, in fact, may be considered as pre-requisite for most forms of effective learning.

So how will we as teachers identify whether or not our students are being truly reflective? A reflective learner will look back at prior learning experiences (both those that they consider to have been successful and, at a more advanced level, those that were less successful) in order to learn lessons for the future. They will be thoughtful in approach and appreciate the need for objectivity. Reflective learners will have the maturity and strength of character to see failure as an opportunity to learn for the future and, because of this, readily seek advice from others about their performance and, crucially, how they can improve for the next time.

Engaging students in self-assessment and peer-assessment opportunities could provide a good benchmark for measuring their reflectiveness as could the way in which they respond to formative assessments and targets set by the teacher. Many of the skills and a significant amount of the knowledge within ASK seeks to develop reflectiveness and self-awareness of the learner.

## Picture this...

Probably the most straightforward way of introducing learning-to-learn into the classroom is to include a *meta-learning debrief* into the plenary phase of the lesson. This might take a variety of different forms, and further strategies will be discussed in the next section, but the simplest approach is to ask the students questions, not just about *what* they have learned but also about *how* they have learned it and the explicit learning skills they have developed.

• • • • • • • • • • • • • • • • • • • • • • • • • • • • • • • • • • • • • • • • • • • • • • • • • • • • • • • • •

Hopefully, the above descriptions of individual ASK attitudes have illustrated that the sub-skills or learning-to-learn objectives and outcomes, while naturally belonging under one of the seven skill headings of ASK, could alternatively be grouped in a meaningful way under the heading of one or more attitudes. This multi-dimensional aspect to the ASK curriculum lends cohesion and reflects the complexity of the learning process and of neural connections within the brain itself!

# The skills and knowledge of effective learners

By offering detailed content for learning skills and knowledge, we believe that learning-to-learn makes more sense and is more manageable in the day to day of teaching. Teachers can identify and make real progress with specific learning skills and knowledge in individual lessons, confident that they are empowering students within their subject and putting in place skills and knowledge useful for other subjects.

As Chapter 1 illustrated, ASK is made up of the following seven learning-to-learn skills and knowledge areas.

| **UNDERSTANDING SELF AS A LEARNER** | Understanding the learning process<br>Developing and sustaining motivation<br>Developing self-knowledge |
|---|---|

This skill and knowledge area has strong links with the attitudes:

- reflectiveness
- responsiveness
- resourcefulness.

A student who knows their potential as a learner must have a sound understanding of the learning process and how they learn best. They establish strategies to keep going when the going gets tough and understand the principles of learning-to-learn, applying them to maximise their potential.

Trying to break the habit of keeping learning and managing learning a secret, this skill and knowledge area opens up the learning process so that students can have a greater understanding and involvement in it, using it to assess and develop their own performance.

Understanding the learning process stresses the importance of sharing theory and knowledge about learning with students, in particular the learning-to-learn curriculum.

Developing and sustaining motivation recognises that students often feel like giving up and offers suggestions and strategies to make sure students can see the value of what they are doing and keep on task.

Developing self-knowledge explores ways students can apply their knowledge about learning to their understanding of themselves in order to learn independently and still make progress.

| **LEARNING WITH AND FROM OTHERS** | Understanding group dynamics and managing relationships<br>Assessing and making progress<br>Communicating ideas |
|---|---|

This skill and knowledge area has strong links with the attitudes:

- reciprocity
- responsiveness
- resourcefulness.

A student who successfully learns with and from others has a confident ability to manage groups and can, when necessary, select the best type of group and understand the need for different roles within different types of groups. They are able to share assessment with their peers and accept feedback from others. They present their ideas in original ways and show skill and flair in engaging their audience's attention.

Highlighting the reality of the day-to-day difficulties of learning together, this skill and knowledge area attempts to break down the intricacies of 'group-work' and working with others into useful, practical strategies that teachers can use to help students maximise the effectiveness of some of the most frequently used classroom strategies.

Understanding group dynamics focuses on managing personal relationships and develops students' abilities to behave assertively and negotiate.

Assessing and making progress looks to provide ways for students to assess the work of their peers against relevant assessment criteria and give both formative and summative comments using the most appropriate oral and non-verbal language in feedback.

Communicating ideas recognises the need for students to be able to present material and ideas effectively in a variety of different settings, paying particular attention to audience and purpose.

| **PLANNING** | Turning objectives into actions<br>Monitoring<br>Reflecting, evaluating and re-planning |
| --- | --- |

This skill and knowledge area has strong links with the attitudes:
- resourcefulness
- reflectiveness
- responsiveness.

A student who is able to plan effectively has an organized and controlled approach to learning, making sure tasks are clearly understood before they are undertaken. They are aware of what is expected and have an idea of how to reach their intended outcome.

Knowing that students are often keen to get straight on with a task without thinking through their approach to it or the different parts of it, this skill and knowledge area makes planning a central part of the learning process from start to finish.

Turning objectives into actions stresses the importance of teaching students to imagine and visualise the end before beginning to plan, as well as breaking tasks down, prioritising and managing deadlines.

Monitoring reminds the student of their responsibilities to manage distractions and assess their progress against deadlines and criteria, advising a positive approach throughout.

Evaluating links planning with the areas of Thinking and Adapting, stressing the importance of reviewing and making adjustments and changes to present and future planning.

| **INVESTIGATING RESOURCES** | Locating and selecting<br>Displaying and recording<br>Assimilating |
| --- | --- |

This skill and knowledge area has strong links with the attitudes:
- resourcefulness
- reciprocity
- reflectiveness.

A student who investigates resources thoroughly has an awareness of the resources available to them and is able to select what is relevant and discard what is irrelevant. They use resources to extend their learning and are capable of checking their understanding of their resources. They have a sophisticated reading of texts, in particular media texts, showing awareness of social and historical context.

Recognising the problems faced by students in an information age, this skill and knowledge area attempts to offer ways to manage resources and check their relevance.

Locating and selecting suggests ways to help students become aware of the range of resources at their disposal and to develop students' abilities to assess the resources relevance and use.

Displaying and recording offers methods and strategies to make the right kind of notes about the relevant sections of resources and texts.

Assimilating stresses the importance for the student of personalising their note-taking and being able to effectively summarise information, showing awareness of the origin of a resource.

21

| **DEVELOPING MEMORY** | Understanding memory<br>Using memory effectively<br>Transferring learning |
|---|---|

This skill and knowledge area has strong links with the attitudes:
- resilience
- responsiveness
- resourcefulness
- reflectiveness.

A student who uses their memory well is able to retain information and knowledge efficiently and recall it when it is needed. They manage to organise their learning and recall and to apply what is relevant for a particular task at a particular time.

Challenging the assumption that it is simply something we can all do, this skill and knowledge area attempts to teach students how to use their memories more effectively by explaining its possibilities and limitations.

Understanding memory explains the basics of memory, its functions and capabilities, and looks at ways to help students understand them.

Using memory effectively suggests ways to help students use their memory and to select appropriate strategies for retaining learning.

Transferring learning focuses on the important challenge of organising and managing memory and explores ways to access and recall relevant knowledge to apply to make progress in new learning experiences.

| **THINKING** | Questioning<br>Analysing<br>Synthesising |
|---|---|

This skill and knowledge area has strong links with all the attitudes apart from reciprocity.

A student who is an effective thinker understands the importance of an individual's own thinking in learning and making progress. They enjoy the challenge offered by trying to learn new things and want to test their ideas and stretch themselves.

Aware of the fact that thinking can easily be assumed or taken for granted, this skill and knowledge area recognises the complex nature of thinking and tries to identify the similarities and differences within thinking across different subjects.

Questioning sets out to ensure students know when and how to use different types of questions for different purposes.

Analysing offers students models to use to go deeper into their thinking and understanding. It also stresses the importance of finding patterns and alternative meanings in things.

Synthesising encourages students to group ideas and make connections between them and also between new and old ideas.

| ADAPTING | Making observations<br>Dealing with feelings<br>Learning from mistakes and making progress |
|---|---|

This skill and knowledge area has strong links with the attitudes:
- responsiveness
- reflectiveness
- resilience.

A student who can adapt will learn from their past experiences and prior knowledge. They regularly reflect and evaluate on their learning and their own performance and, having drawn conclusions, will seek to make the necessary changes to ensure progress.

Understanding the difficulty many students find in making the necessary changes to make progress, this skill and knowledge area maps out the journey students need to take in order to be able to make changes to the way they approach their learning.

Making observations highlights the importance of students being aware of the way they learn and selecting the right strategies for a specific learning task.

Dealing with feelings has strong links with 'Developing and sustaining motivation' in 'Understanding self as learner' and tries to ensure students have the right approach and mind-set to be able to use different forms of feedback and assessment to make progress.

Learning from mistakes and making progress builds on the work from Transferring Learning in Developing Memory and provides ideas and stimulus for ensuring that students have strategies to learn from failure, build on success and make the necessary changes to be effective independent learners.

This comprehensive list represents skills and knowledge central to and accordant with all areas of learning for life. With the five attitudes under-pinning the curriculum, ASK offers a model of development for independent learning inside and outside of the school and for lifelong learning.

As with any curriculum, it is important to map out precisely what it is that needs to be taught. This means attempting to break down the headline of learning skills in order to classify the skills and knowledge needed for development into practical sub-headings that are both meaningful and useful to teachers. It is important to mention at this point that there is an obvious tension between the need to divide learning-to-learn into workable and manageable chunks and the recognition and acceptance that all the divisions are ultimately interlinked. There will therefore be parts of one skill and knowledge area that some teachers may feel would be better placed under another heading or that a heading itself should be named differently or grouped with something else. Seven is not a magic number, it could just as easily be many more or one or two less. ASK originally began as six attitudes and fifteen areas of skills and knowledge, but over time as it was tried and tested by staff across the whole school it was refined. In another institution in another place, it may morph again.

We feel strongly that this type of discussion and debate should take place at all levels of the school. The mapping-out process of a learning-centred curriculum is a valuable whole-school exercise as it forces teachers to identify the barriers to learning faced by the students they teach who are unable to make progress in their individual subject areas. Asking teachers to focus not on difficulties with their subject and its content, but on difficulties that arise as a result of poorly demonstrated learning, brings the relevant learning to the forefront.

The process of teachers focusing on learning and assessment of learning rather than on teaching is an essential starting point in making learning-to-learn a central whole-school focus. It unites everybody under the same subject. For once, teachers are not in competition with one another. Instead, they share a goal and have a shared language with which to express their shared aims and outcomes. Furthermore, there is an understanding that what students learn in one subject is of vital importance to how they can learn in another.

The transfer of learning skills and knowledge is a central part of ASK, and its success at a whole-school level depends upon it. This said, research is beginning to show that the delivery of knowledge about learning and providing opportunities for the development of learning-to-learn skills by individual teachers in their own lessons alone does still have a positive effect upon students' performance in their studies in that subject. Learning-to-learn makes a difference at whatever level it takes place at within a school. How a school ensures that a transfer of learning skills takes place is something for consideration and discussion at all levels of school leadership and we have apportioned sections of Part 2 and Part 3 for further discussion of this.

It is worth mentioning that in trying to span the breadth of what constitutes effective independent learning and, more generally, the learning process, the different areas of the curriculum naturally vary in their size, profundity and weightiness. In addition, some areas, such as Memorising and Planning, are at their heart fairly clear and concrete, whereas others such as Thinking and Adapting are far looser and more abstract.

In our experience, neither the concrete nor the abstract elements of learning are taught very effectively. More often than not, there is an enormous presumption on the part of the teacher that students know how to learn and have developed learning strategies to use. Concrete skills such as memorising and note-taking are taken as a given and little or no time is spent discussing them and sharing ideas about them. The more abstract concepts such as listening, questioning and thinking are referred to constantly, but, somewhat ironically, without much thought or preparation and with no framework offered to allow students an insight into further enquiry, understanding or development. The questions, 'Are you listening?', 'I want you to think about this?' or 'Any questions?' are synonymous with nearly all lessons, and yet theory about and development of all three skills is lacking.

One reason for this may be that teachers themselves do not feel 'expert' enough to teach these areas. It is true that in teaching students how to learn, there are demands on teachers to get to know more about the theory of learning and to be creative in their teaching of it, but we would also stress that the most important role the teacher can play in learning-to-learn is to adopt the model of an inquisitive, independent learner themselves. Good learners do not pretend to know all the answers, but they make inquiries, exploring and discovering new ways to discover new things. ASK offers both real theory and ideas for teaching learning-to-learn as well as laying out a model for effective learning generally.

Here is an example from science.

# Using ASK in science

### Making enquiries about memory

A science teacher frustrated at students' poor ability to retain and recall information in her subject asked a group of language teachers how they made sure students could remember new vocabulary at will. She noted that most language teachers explicitly coached the students in the strategies of *repetition and *hide and seek.

### Transferring the skills and knowledge and making it explicit

The teacher then chose the topic of teaching the PH scale, which required a lot of memory recall, to begin building on what the students already knew about memory and helping them to apply it in her subject. She discussed what the students already knew about memory and found that she had to actually mention their language lessons to enable them to discuss their prior knowledge.

### Practising the skills and establishing the knowledge

The class then practised the memory strategies on tasks not directly related to the subject, such as tube lines, shopping lists and the colours in the rainbow. The teacher also introduced new memory skills called *association and *mnemonics.

### Applying the skills and embedding the knowledge to the subject

She then introduced the topic and explained what the class needed to be able to do at the end of the unit. The class agreed that memory was going to be very important and groups decided which memory strategy they were going to select to use. Most chose the strategy they had used to retain and recall the colours of the rainbow as they felt there was a similarity with the science task. They then applied the memory strategy to their learning throughout the topic.

### Reviewing and evaluating

The class tested their memories regularly as they worked through the unit. They reflected upon whether they had chosen a 'good' strategy and considered whether there were other strategies they could have used that would have been just as effective. Finally, they made judgements about topics in other subjects where they could use their knowledge about memory.

*Assessment*

The teacher noted that six months later in the end-of-year science exam there was a noticeable improvement in her students' general recall and, in particular, in their response to questions about the PH scale.

* Information about the memory strategies mentioned here can be found in Chapter 8.

# 3 Reflection and meta-learning

*'It is by logic that we prove, but by intuition that we discover.'*

POINCARÉ

*'The world we have made as a result of the level of thinking we have done thus far creates problems that we cannot solve at the same level (of consciousness) at which we have created them … We shall require a substantially new manner of thinking if humankind is to survive.'*

ALBERT EINSTEIN

## COMING UP IN THIS CHAPTER:

▶ Meta-learning and why it is important.
▶ Ten ways of putting meta-learning into practice.

## What do we mean by meta-learning?

Meta-learning is at the heart of our ASK curriculum and runs through it like the rings through the trunk of a tree. While the word may sound strange, the concept it describes is an essential one. For meta-learning is *explicitly* learning about the learning process itself. The phrase increasingly being used to describe it is 'learning-to-learn'.

Our students learn about the learning process because we as teachers challenge them to *think* about the learning process and *reflect* not just on *what* they have learned, that is to say the traditional subject content, but *how* they have learned it by referring explicitly to aspects of knowledge and skills of the learning process itself.

## Why is meta-learning important in helping students learn how to learn?

Meta-learning is crucial in empowering students to become more effective, independent and, thus, lifelong learners. The knowledge of, and ability to select, the best way to learn (whether alone or with others) and to select the most appropriate resources is another stepping stone towards becoming an independent learner. The ability to define and *reflect* on one's own personal learning 'toolkit' and form powerful relationships with other learners (both peers and adults) are further benefits of incorporating meta-learning into a student's experience. Arguably, the most important benefit of engaging with meta-learning is that, through continuous reflection, self-evaluation and setting one's own learning development targets, a learner is most likely to make continuous progress. Here we see, yet again, how reflectiveness is strongly linked with meta-learning and learning-to-learn as a whole.

# Strategies for meta-learning in the classroom: a ten-step plan

Listed below are ten practical strategies for introducing meta-learning into the classroom. Some are concrete and straightforward to introduce with minimal effort, while others are 'deeper' and could require more commitment to change the ethos in the classroom.

## Strategy 1: Be explicit

Make explicit and display the ASK (learning-to-learn) objectives alongside the subject-specific objectives at the beginning of a lesson or learning episode. Students may be questioned, if appropriate, as to where they may have met these learning skills and attitudes before: either in other curriculum areas or outside of the school environment altogether, in that strange and unfamiliar place referred to by (some) teachers as 'real life'!

## Strategy 2: Meta-learning review

Towards the end of a lesson (possibly as part of the 'plenary'), conduct a meta-learning review. In other words, challenge students to reflect upon, and possibly answer questions about, the learning skills they have used and developed in the lesson. This is likely to take only a few minutes and may not need to be done every lesson but frequently enough to create a sense of continuity and progression.

The meta-learning review is probably the most straightforward way of introducing ASK and 'learning-to-learn' into the classroom.

## Strategy 3: Make connections

During a lesson, as and when opportunities arise, comment on generic learning skills or attitudes and dispositions the students are required to use in order to be effective. Communicate the impression that the learning process is just as important to the students as the subject itself.

## Strategy 4: Encourage transfer

Encourage students to keep some form of *learning journal* in which to record their knowledge and skills about the learning process. This might help students to *transfer* their ASK skills to other areas of the curriculum.

## Strategy 5: 'This is because…'

Justify your lesson plan! Explain to the students why you have chosen to approach their learning in this way. When events do not go according to plan, think and re-plan out loud with the class. If you are feeling particularly brave, you might ask the students to suggest alternative strategies for you. At the end of a lesson or topic, ask the class to comment on the effectiveness of the methodology. You can ask them to *reflect* on their responses to different learning activities and so develop their awareness of personal learning styles.

## Strategy 6: Enrich the learning environment

Display *learning words* around the room in the same way that you have technical language and keywords from your subject. It is important that students build the vocabulary of learning. Model the use of technical words yourself and expect students to use the correct vocabulary.

## Strategy 7: Speak the language of learning

Frequently ask students to explain *how* they arrived at an answer or *how* they approached a particular task. Ask questions such as, 'What was your strategy?' and 'Is there another/better way of doing this?' Value the *processes* of thinking as much as the *outcomes* or products by devoting time to talk about them.

## Strategy 8: Smart people learn from mistakes

In the learning-to-learn classroom, and even in the school as a whole, it is important for teachers to model and communicate clearly the message that it is smart to make mistakes and learn from them. This will have direct implications for the language used by the teacher while teaching (particularly during whole-class question-and-answer sessions) as well as affecting interactions between teachers and students and between teachers themselves.

## Strategy 9: 'Ask questions first, accept later…'

Change the student's attitude to knowledge: rather than certainty and indisputable fact, try to present the acquisition of knowledge as something to be *questioned*. Encourage students to challenge everything and not just to take your word (or anyone else's for that matter) for anything without asking questions such as:

- Why?
- How do you know?
- Are there any other ways we could do this?

## Strategy 10: Personalise!

For the truly confident and brave! Sooner or later, students will have to practise the skills of planning and managing their own learning if they are to become truly self-sufficient and independent learners. This means providing learning opportunities that give students:

- a chance to determine their own pace and challenge
- choice
- an opportunity to investigate and research independently
- an opportunity to negotiate their learning strategy.

# PART 2

## How to teach it

# Introduction to Part 2

The chapters in Part 2 cover all the skills and knowledge areas from the learning-to-learn curriculum at Villiers. They suggest what we hope are imaginative and engaging ways into these areas.

Although it is perfectly possible to develop an established skill and knowledge in one particular area in an intensive and concentrated way with students, we recognise that it is more likely that teachers will dip in and out of each area and will link them to what they are currently teaching.

For this reason, we have tried to lay out each skill and knowledge area with as much useful detail as possible and in a user-friendly manner. Each chapter in Part 2 is divided into the following sections:

- *Introduction* – an introduction to the area.
- *Skills and knowledge breakdown* – a breakdown of sub-skills and possible outcomes that a teacher might plan to develop in students when concentrating on the area.
- *Learning episodes* – two detailed learning episodes designed to teach the development of key aspects of the area, including objectives, overview, suggested resources, starter activities, main teaching ideas, meta-learning reviews and ideas for transferring the skill.
- *Building in progression* – a list of statements for teacher assessment and student self-assessment to track and to plan for the development of progression.
- *What the teachers say* – transcripts of teachers describing their experiences of teaching the area in their subject.
- *Taking it further* – ideas for further development of the area.

As already mentioned, the skills and knowledge we have identified as making up ASK are inextricably linked both with each other and with the attitudes. There are many crossovers and there is much reference of one skill and knowledge within another. We think this is as it should be.

It is perfectly realistic to be teaching something in your subject that requires you to develop a number of the skills in order for the students to effectively learn the subject matter. This is where the expertise of the teacher is at its most crucial, as, just like the English teacher having to decide to concentrate only on the development of complex sentences even though there are glaring problems with the paragraphing, spelling and use of tense, the learning-to-learn teacher must decide which is the priority area for the particular piece of subject area study.

Our advice is not to worry too much about the skills and knowledge you are not developing but you feel you should be; instead, remember that each skill will need to be covered many different times, in many different subjects and over a long time before it is in any way mastered. Each learning-to-learn experience is itself an important piece in a jigsaw puzzle that will take a lifetime to complete.

The learning episodes explained in detail throughout Part 2 are by no means definitive plans for the successful teaching and effective development of learning-to-learn in the classroom. They are ideas to take as a starting point for introducing and then developing and integrating the teaching of the skills and knowledge from our ASK curriculum.

In our experience of leading the development of learning-to-learn, we have found that a lot of discussion has arisen among staff around the issue of whether their learning-to-learn teaching should be totally separate from their usual subject lessons or whether they should teach learning-to-learn within their subject content.

We have always been clear that the most successful teaching of learning-to-learn is to do both. The reasons for this can be summed up as follows.

Attitudes, skills and knowledge about learning-to-learn sometimes need to be taught explicitly from the subject content of the lesson so that students see that learning is a separate skill from the subject itself. This is particularly important when a skill is being initially introduced. It can be difficult to develop new knowledge or make progress in an area if it is not explained in its own separate context.

Keeping learning-to-learn explicit at times makes it easier to highlight its relevance to effective learning generally and its transferability.

At the same time, the attitudes, skills and knowledge also need to be linked with the subjects the students are studying because that is where they will need to use them. Equally, the requirements of a particular area of learning-to-learn will be different in different subjects and need to evolve within the different contexts they will be used in.

Recently, we interviewed some staff from the school to discuss their own progress with learning-to-learn and one particular teacher was very clear about the process they had developed to teach learning-to-learn. We have included it, not as a model, but as an example of one teacher's understanding of the need for explicit and integrated teaching and learning of learning-to-learn:

'After I have introduced a new topic or a new learning objective and proposed the activity I plan to run, I will always discuss with the students which learning-to-learn skills are going to be important. Sometimes I'll decide, other times I deliberately leave it to them. I try to run an explicit learning-to-learn activity regularly to develop their knowledge and understanding of the skill we are focusing on. This often lasts about 15 minutes, but can last a whole lesson. Then, while I run my subject-specific activity, I ensure that the students are continuing to stay aware of the learning skills we focused on and, wherever possible, are applying them. I always run some sort of subject-specific plenary, but will always keep five minutes to also run a meta-learning plenary, which is often a series of questions, but can sometimes be filling in a survey, diary or self-assessment sheet. I can't always fit this into one lesson – in fact sometimes that process will take the best part of a week – but it works because as much as possible I stick to it and the students become used to learning about learning as well as my subject.'

Another useful idea we have used to help staff deliver learning-to-learn more effectively is to get them to use what we refer to as the *split screen model*. This is a good visual metaphor to illustrate the last point made by the teacher above; namely, that learning-to-learn means that students and learners are learners both of their subject and of learning.

The split screen model also manages to capture the nature of learning-to-learn and its relationship to the subject. Both need to be developed separately at times, but success overall requires the use of learning-to-learn to enable more effective learning and progress in the subject. The split screen model is a useful image to take into planning the teaching of learning-to-learn.

| ENGLISH | LEARNING-TO-LEARN |
|---|---|
| **Intended learning outcomes:** | **Intended learning outcomes:** |
| Students to identify some of the techniques used to create effective imagery in poetry. | *Using Memory Effectively* <br> Students to apply effective memory strategy to retain terminology about techniques and their definitions. |
| Students to be able to use knowledge of these techniques to explore effects created by different writers' use of imagery. | *Transferring Learning* <br> Students to know how, when and where to apply knowledge about techniques to new learning. |

**Example of a split screen model**

# A word about progression

As with everything else you teach, you will want the students to make progress with learning-to-learn. It goes without saying that it is important to have strategies to plan progression into the learning-to-learn experiences of the students and to have criteria for assessment.

Part of the resources in each chapter in Part 2 include what we have named 'Progression Statements'. They are written from the point of view of the learner and attempt to describe two levels of the skills and knowledge in each of the areas of the curriculum.

One method of ensuring progression, in lesson planning at least, is initially to use specific statements from the 'basic end' of the statements as the intended outcomes of particular learning and then aim to progress onto the statements from the 'more established end' as the skills and knowledge are developed further. This also helps to focus the development of learning-to-learn onto quite specific and manageable areas and to break down the teaching of the curriculum into bite-size pieces.

Another helpful way of viewing the progression statements is to think of each statement as a clear learning outcome to be used as a way for you and the students to assess their progress.

As a final note before Part 2, we have learned that the teacher of learning-to-learn must not only become skilled at building learning-to-learn into their lesson plans in imaginative and useful ways, but they must also become good at spotting and maximising the opportunities to develop learning-to-learn that arise from the lessons. The last chapter of Part 2 is slightly different from Chapters 4–10. It suggests how teachers can include a variety of generic learning-to-learn techniques in their lessons in order to encourage students to take ownership of their own learning. You may want to start by reading Chapter 11 before going into the details of the chapters dealing with specific skills.

# 4 Understanding yourself as a learner

*'I'm afraid you're not making much progress in this subject.*
*Why do you think that is?'*
*'You're the teacher, you tell me!'*

## Introduction

In his classic film *Modern Times*, Charlie Chaplin clearly illustrates the de-motivating effect of working on a factory conveyor belt – busy all day doing but without any awareness, understanding or ownership of the process or purpose of the work. He was excluded from knowing anything about the process he was involved in. He was not consulted about any decisions and had no input about what was done when, or how something was to be achieved. It is difficult to care, be motivated or want to change something if you do not know anything about it or feel part of it.

Sound familiar?

If we are honest, we as teachers make most of the decisions and hold most of the control in our classrooms. We decide when something is studied and how it is to be taught. We decide whether the students work in groups or individually and we decide the tasks they will be set. We decide the learning objectives, outcomes, the tests and content of the tests and we decide the environment the students will learn in. Why do we do this? Well, we have a list of very good reasons for this autocracy: we have a curriculum to get through, we are the subject experts, we have data on the class that informs us about how they best learn and, finally, if we left it to the kids to decide, nothing would get done, they would not have a clue what to do. And why is this? Well, they are not in the know. And so it becomes a vicious circle.

But could we be missing a golden opportunity? We want students to make progress and recognise that they ultimately are the only ones who can do this. We know from research that it is difficult to bring change about without at the very least shared ownership and understanding between both teacher and student.

A learning-to-learn school is a school where everyone is learning together, teachers and students: it is a shared process. You cannot be in charge of your own learning unless you have a sound understanding of how you as an individual best learn. Teachers often report the difficulty of discussing learning with students they teach because of the students' ignorance of the teaching and learning process. Yet is this surprising if from the choosing of a scheme of work through to the planning of lesson through to the teaching, assessment and feedback, the students are kept entirely separate from the explicit process. The first time we talk to students about their learning and ask for their input it is bound to be a superficial discussion at best. Yet if we keep going with the discussions and the involvement, then slowly, over time, as their confidence, their vocabulary and their experience increase, so the competence, expertise and quality of their involvement will grow to such a level that it is not impossible to imagine them playing a full and, at times, independent part in the decisions about what they need to learn and achieve and how they learn and achieve it.

The original purpose of ASK was to develop more independently motivated students who have a greater understanding of the learning process and of how they themselves learn; meaning that they are more capable of taking an active role in their learning, in their lessons and in school life in general. This means reaching a point where teachers are able to introduce a topic, to plan with the students what the relevant aims and objectives might be, to get the students to plan how those objectives could be met, to decide what activities would be effective based on the purpose of the task and to decide what the learning outcome will be.

This first skill and knowledge area from the ASK curriculum is the first step to gaining that expertise.

## Attitude development

| | |
|---|---|
| Resourcefulness | ✓ ✓ ✓ ✓ |
| Resilience | ✓ ✓ ✓ |
| Responsiveness | ✓ ✓ ✓ ✓ ✓ |
| Reciprocity | ✓ |
| Reflectiveness | ✓ ✓ ✓ ✓ |

# Skills and knowledge breakdown

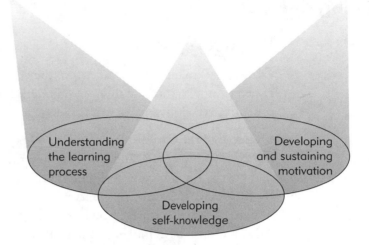

## Understanding the learning process

▷ Be aware of the learning-to-learn curriculum and how it fits together and that each part is needed to make up the whole

▷ Know that during learning, performance can get worse before it gets better

▷ Know some ways of talking about learning styles

▷ Explore new thinking on intelligence

▷ Set targets to build on strengths and eliminate weaknesses

## Developing and sustaining motivation

▷ Use the language of responsibility

▷ Recognise personal strengths and weaknesses

▷ Celebrate strengths

▷ Use positive affirmations

▷ Visualise a successful outcome

▷ Explain the causes and effects of stress

▷ Use a range of strategies to cope with stress

▷ Identify long-term goals

▷ Set achievable short-term targets

▷ Create positive inner dialogue

▷ Know how to turn weaknesses into strengths

## Developing self-knowledge

▷ Work within personal concentration span

▷ Choose techniques to suit personal learning styles and sensory preferences

▷ Know learning styles framework. Minimum: VAK

▷ Know multiple intelligence theory

▷ Reflect regularly on learning experiences to build a picture of personal learning styles and aptitudes

▷ Make study choices in school and at home based on awareness of personal profile

▷ Set targets to build on strengths and eliminate weaknesses

▷ Conduct regular self-evaluation

# Learning episodes

## Learning episode 1

**Objective:** to introduce students to the concepts of intelligence and expertise and to increase their own understanding of how to become more expert about a particular topic.

**Overview:** the starter offers a chance to explore and compare intelligence and be skilful at something. The main learning episode explores the idea that everybody can gain expertise in their learning at school and beyond. By the end of the lesson, students should have a greater understanding of how to develop a deeper knowledge and skill in a specific area or topic. They may also have increased their confidence in their own learning.

### Suggested resources

- It is useful for the starter to have cartoons of babies and adults, similar to those in Figure 4.1.
- It is also useful for the starter to show images of the brain; for example, see Figure 4.2.

**Figure 4.1 Cartoons of adults and babies for comparison**

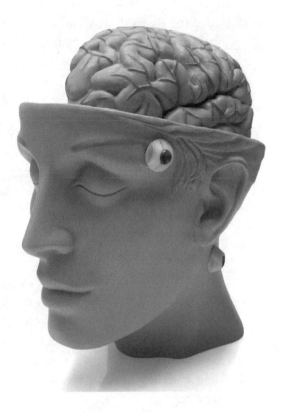

**Figure 4.2  Image of the brain**

## Detailed description of learning episode 1

### Starter

1   Explore the concepts of intelligence and expertise. You could do some or all of the following:
    ■   Explore the things an adult can do that a baby cannot, how we learn how to do them and where students think learning takes place. (The suggested resources shown opposite can be useful visual stimuli throughout this discussion.)
    ■   Explore the concept of intelligence using examples of famous people such as Albert Einstein and Leonardo Da Vinci.
    ■   Compare this 'intelligence' with the expertise of celebrities such as David Beckham and Sachin Tendulkar.

### Main learning episode

2   The main lesson explores the idea that everybody can gain expertise in their learning at school. You will need to choose a topic, either of universal interest or from within your own subject. The remainder of this episode uses the topic of human fertilisation as an example.

3   Explain that groups of four have 15 minutes to become as expert as possible about how the human egg becomes fertilised and how the foetus develops in the early stages of pregnancy.

4   Give the class a short written test about the topic that has a wide variety of questions and that takes into account the information that could be obtained from each resource used in the next step. Collect in their answers.

5   Explain that each group will have a different resource to use to become more expert, before taking the same test again. For example, a short video about the topic, a school text book, a useful website, a leaflet from a doctor's surgery, spending the time talking with the teacher, a variety of photos, relevant chapters from a self-help book for pregnant women, such as *What to Expect when you're Expecting* or *The Rough Guide to Pregnancy*, and articles and/or interviews from a magazine about pregnancy.

6   After the group have 'studied' their resource, discuss the pros and cons of their resource.

7   Depending on time, ask groups to select one or two more resources to use that is most likely to be helpful now. You may want to organise this so that the groups change the type of resource they are using – predominately visual resources groups get more auditory or kinaesthetic ones, and vice versa.

8   Give the class the same written test as before, again collecting in their answers.

9   If you have time, ask the groups to prepare a short presentation about the topic for a group of their peers who they presume know very little about this subject.

10  Ask them to take the same written test again, collecting in their answers. After the lesson has ended, assess the three tests taken by each student and give them feedback about how their results have changed.

### Meta-learning

1   Ask the students to identify which resources they found most helpful and why.

2   Explore with the students whether it was the quality of the resource or their response to the type of the resource or both that made it helpful or not.

3   Ask the students to review their progress in the tests and discuss reasons for it.

## Learning episode 2

**Objective:** to develop students' awareness of assessment, to give students real experiences of assessing themselves, and to set work related to assessment and targeted at making progress.

**Overview:** the starter phase asks students to assess their own skill levels in certain fields. The main part of the learning experience focuses on increasing and developing students' awareness of assessment by looking at

JOB VACANCY FOR:

# INFORMATION MANAGER AT DISNEYLAND

We here at Euro-Disney in Paris have a wonderful vacancy for an experienced, committed and enthusiastic young person, who has a wide knowledge of Disney stories.

**You will be working on a variety of different jobs all over the park so you will need to be skilled in many different areas.**

You will need to have your summer holidays free and be full of energy.

**You need to be literate and have mature oral skills as well as enjoying a challenge.**

*To apply please send a letter of application to our General Manager at:*

**Euro-Disney, Paris, 2010**

**Figure 4.3  Job advertisement**

14, My House
My Street
My Town
MY1 1YM

Dear Disney

I saw the thing in the paper and thought to myself, "I could do that easy", I can do a lot of languages and like talking to people. I know lots about your films and cartoons and we've done them in school. I never stop running around so I must have lots of energy and my mum says I'd be dead good at helping the people that come to your place because I did the same sort of thing at the play-park round the corner from my house. I'm not doing nothing all holidays and I'd be quite bored otherwise. Give us a ring or write me note if you want me to come and do the job.

Cheers
Love From

Harpreet

**Figure 4.4  Job application letter**

the required skills for a variety of tasks. Students need to use their knowledge about useful formative assessment, as well as their experiences of learning and making progress, to help others improve and to set their own assessment criteria.

## Suggested resources

It is useful for the main part of the learning experience to use job advertisements and applications to assess skills; for example, see Figures 4.3 and 4.4.

■ It is useful to give students vocabulary or a model to help them assess themselves; for example, *I am fantastic at…, I am good at…, I am OK at…, I have difficulties at….* Alternatively, they could use a number range or scale or a diagram of some sorts.

## Detailed description of learning episode 2

### Starter

1 Ask the students to list three of their strengths and three of their weaknesses. Follow this by asking them to decide upon their ideal job and then to brainstorm the three to five key skills that a person would need to be good at to do the job well.

### Main learning episode

2 Hand out a simple job advertisement (see Figure 4.3 for suggestion) and discuss and list the skills needed to be a successful applicant.

3 Focus on skills of communication and literacy from the list and display copies of a prepared poorly constructed letter of application for the job (see Figure 4.4 for suggestion). Explain that the class should assess the letter in pairs and prepare formative feedback and assessment that would be useful in helping the pretend applicant improve their job application letter. Explain that the pairs are to present the feedback orally.

4 Discuss the principles of effective feedback; for example, positive before negative, constructive forward-focusing criticism with practical suggestions for improvement.

5 Make time to listen to a few pairs present their feedback and evaluate the quality of the feedback with the class.

6 Now set the class the following task:
*Prepare a short teaching and learning experience with the aim of developing the formal letter-writing skills of a group of students with the current letter-writing ability of the pretend applicant.*
(The task is quite demanding, so try putting pairs together, preferably with mixed ability in different skills such as presenting, writing, and learning with and from others.)

7   It may be useful to remind the students of learning episode 1 and to share students' experiences of being taught skills such as this in lessons. Discuss the students' views about the successes and failures of these teaching and learning experiences.

8   Share with the class the criteria you will use for assessing how successful the teaching and learning episodes are at achieving their aim.

9   Give the pairs sufficient time to prepare and then arrange for some or all the presentations to be given.

10  After each presentation, take time to allow the class to assess and give feedback.

### Meta-learning

1   After step 2, ask the students to assess their own ability in those skills. They should provide examples or evidence of where they have demonstrated particular levels of aptitude in the skills.

2   Compare with the class the results of the two exercises in the starter and ask students to review their job choices.

3   At the end of the main learning experience when each pair has presented, take feedback from the class about how helpful their feedback would be for the pretend applicant. (Concentrate on key areas such as highlighting areas of strength and weakness, or the quality and practicality of suggested strategies to improve and target setting.)

4   Discuss with students their experiences of preparing the teaching and learning objective and encourage pairs to evaluate their performance and success in achieving their aim.

## Transferring the skill and knowledge

- In geography: during geographical investigations, such as exploring coastal regions.
- In science: after carrying out an experiment with the class, ask them to review what they have learned and how they have learned it.
- In PE: to help develop more self-awareness in students about how to develop individual skills within particular sports.

## Progression statement

When planning learning-to-learn, you will want to build progression into your schemes of learning and learning plans. In this section, we have described progression as we see it and hope this will help you map out learning-to-learn as a continuous part of your curriculum.

| | |
|---|---|
| **Developing self-knowledge** | I often identify the skills I am using to learn something as well as the information or content that I am learning. <br> I have a good idea of my strengths as a learner and want to build on them. <br> I think about what I have learned and use it to help me in my homework and in other lessons. <br> I understand the different ways that I learn and know which are my preferred learning styles. <br> I make effective choices about the way in which I learn something. <br> I use skills I have learned in other subjects to help me in my learning. |
| **Developing and sustaining motivation** | I try to plan and manage my workload so that I do not end up with overly busy or stressful times. <br> I am aware of my weaknesses as a learner and have developed ways of coping with them and developing them into strengths. <br> I have several strategies for coping with stress. |
| **Understanding the learning process** | I know that there are many different ways of learning the same thing. <br> I am aware of what is meant by 'meta-cognition' and 'meta-learning'. <br> I understand the following terms: circle time, Brain Gym®, mind mapping. <br> I know about multiple intelligences. <br> I am aware of the following thinking frameworks: Bloom's Taxonomy, Lipman's P4C, DeBono's Thinking Hats, Fisher's Ideas. <br> I always make sure that I am clear about the aim and outcome of what I am trying to learn. |

*As students develop into established learners, their increased understanding and awareness will be reflected as follows.*

| | |
|---|---|
| **Developing self-knowledge** | I am beginning to realise that everybody's brain works differently and that it is important to get to know how mine works. <br> I know that in order to learn successfully I need water, fresh air, enough sleep, regular exercise and a suitable place to work. <br> I talk to my teachers and peers about the different ways that something can be achieved or completed. |
| **Developing and sustaining motivation** | I recognise when I am stressed. <br> I try to imagine a successful outcome to encourage me to keep going when things get difficult. <br> I am beginning to build a list of strategies that help me when I get stuck. |
| **Understanding the learning process** | I make simple connections between the different subjects that I study. <br> I know I can improve my learning, but am not often sure how to do this. <br> I understand what 'learning-to-learn' means. <br> I know what is meant by an intelligence profile. |

*Initially, students may connect to the learning in the following ways.*

## What the teachers say

'The RE homework project is built around the learning-to-learn skills as well as other skills that are RE specific. The students are given maybe eight to ten weeks to complete a project, they hand it in halfway through and then we go through a process where they actually assess following real criteria, so they know what they should be doing to achieve and make progress. Then they mark their own work and they grade their work and they look at what they could do to improve it. To be able to mark and to grade their own work they need a fairly good learning vocabulary. They need to know what certain assessment terms mean. The vocabulary is quite explicit there, and again they're given a whole lesson or two looking at assessment, the process of assessment, what I'm looking for, giving them exemplars and they get to ask questions. This brings them into the learning process and shares with them what might have traditionally been considered the teacher's territory. I mean traditionally, I think, the whole idea of assessment was that we gave them pieces of work that they completed and then we got it back and graded their learning and understanding based on that assessed piece of work, but that doesn't, I don't think, demonstrate learning and understanding in any way. All you have is a completed piece of work. I find that when I share processes with them, they are much more involved and in charge of their learning, and assessment is a part of that learning. I also find that when they come and do a similar piece of work again, it tends to have sunk in a bit more. They're more aware of their learning and take more ownership of it because they're now in control.

Assessment isn't something that's done at the end, it's something that should be done all the time throughout. And in the same way, the learning process isn't something that starts here and ends here, it's a continuous journey. I used to assume a lot of knowledge on the students' behalf, but now I believe that it's essential to share as much theory with them as possible. This is very useful, not just in my subject, but for them to use in different places.'

*Mumin Humayan*, Head of RE and PSHE

## Taking it further

Encourage learners to design their own mark schemes and assessment criteria to match the objectives of what they are being asked to do. As a follow-up activity, ask them to use their criteria to mark their work. Afterwards, invite discussion about how useful and effective their mark schemes were. You may also want them to compare their mark schemes with yours.

After sharing the learning objectives with the class but before going into details about any activities planned to achieve them, ask the students to think about planning the lesson.

Alternatively, after sharing the learning objectives with the class, give the students some thinking time to generate necessary questions that the teacher or peer assessor might ask in order to check whether the learning objectives have been met.

Share stereotypes about learning, such as 'girls are more studious than boys', with the class and allow discussion to develop.

Most important is to keep involving students in the process of their learning and any work from the learning-to-learn curriculum will help them develop their understanding of themselves as learners.

Using the plenary to review what learning skills and attitudes the students have been using and what they might do to continue to develop them will also help. It may prove a good idea to ask the students to make their own 'learning diagram' to illustrate this model of learning and to ask them to use it in other learning experiences.

In our experience, students have benefited most from structured reflection and meta-learning experiences after they have been repeatedly exposed to them. Although there are exceptions, the maxim of 'little and often' seems to have proved effective with most students.

Understanding the learning process does not come as a 'Eureka!' moment overnight, but slowly and over time.

# 5 Learning with and from others

*'Right, I want you in groups of three for the next task.'*
*'Can we work as a group of four, sir?'*
*'No, I said three.'*
*'But why not four?'*
*'Um…'*

## Introduction

In most of the places we spend our time and in most of the things we do, we interact with others. We often rely on them and they rely on us. Convenient as it would sometimes be, we are not individual islands: we are one of many. Those who do well are often those who are skilful at working with and learning from others. But how did they acquire and develop this skill?

For many teachers, group-work and collaborative learning have become regular occurrences in the classroom; either asking students to work in pairs, or threes, with the person or people they are sat next to or to form slightly larger groups with other students, either of their own choice or of the teacher's choice. It is often used as a motivational bribe – *if you're good, I'll let you work in groups* – and the threat of its disappearance can be a useful weapon – *if you don't pay attention now, then I won't let you work in groups and you'll have to do it by yourself.* And that is about as far as the focus on learning with and from others goes.

If we are honest, it often does not live up to its potential. Is the following scenario familiar? You have explained some subject knowledge and set a group task for the class to apply what you hope they have just learned, and yet the students' main preoccupations are about who they want, or do not want, to work with and how many people in all they can work with. Even once the groups have been formed – normally with a lot of direction from the teacher – there are often a number of people off task, either individuals within each group or whole groups. While some sharing of ideas undoubtedly takes place, the pace is often so slow that you wonder if it would have been better getting the class to work individually. It is frustrating, but we persevere because we have been told that, in theory, group-work and collaborative learning allow the exchange of ideas, which actively increases interest, motivation and understanding among group members. In addition to this, it is a great way to share knowledge, generate new ideas, develop critical thinking and check understanding of learning. There is also the fact that it adds energy, enthusiasm

49

and enjoyment to learning. Well, that is the theory, if they could only stop arguing and get onto the task!

Is it any wonder that such methods do not live up to their potential? We spend little time focusing on delivering knowledge about collaborative learning or developing the skills needed to learn effectively with and from others. It is simply seen as a vehicle to get through more subject content, with little or no focus on helping students with the actual collaboration. And it is this part that they so often struggle with – right the way from being comfortable and confident with the students their working with, to the skilful negotiation of compromise and learning from peers. We know from our own experience of working with others on training days or in meetings that the make up and dynamics of the group matters and that there is a real skill to using it effectively for learning.

We believe it is essential that, in preparing young people for the demands of the twenty-first century, we, at the very least, help them develop skills to decide who best to work with for a particular task, to know what makes an efficient group, to be aware of what different roles might be needed to make a group most effective for a particular activity and to distribute roles or share responsibility fairly within the group. Social literacy is surely just as important as any other literacy.

## Attitude development

| | |
|---|---|
| Resourcefulness | ✓ ✓ ✓ |
| Resilience | ✓ ✓ |
| Responsiveness | ✓ ✓ ✓ ✓ |
| Reciprocity | ✓ ✓ ✓ ✓ ✓ |
| Reflectiveness | ✓ ✓ |

# Skills and knowledge breakdown

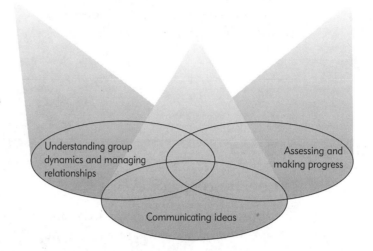

## Understanding group dynamics and managing relationships

▷ Appraise strengths and weaknesses of group members; for example, using 'I' language rather than 'you' language and other techniques to behave assertively

▷ Accept that every action and word is a choice

▷ Negotiate a 'win–win' outcome wherever possible

▷ Explain the difference between aggressive, weak and assertive behaviour

▷ Listen actively and devote total attention

▷ Give oral and non-verbal feedback

▷ Use conflict resolution techniques

▷ Seek first to understand then to be understood

## Assessing and making progress

▷ Compare work with, and make judgements about, assessment criteria

▷ Be rigorous, objective and honest

▷ Explain the difference between subjective and objective judgement

▷ Support all judgements with evidence

▷ Prepare summative and formative feedback when appropriate

▷ Check that all targets are SMART (Specific Measurable Appropriate Realistic Timed) where appropriate

▷ Suggest actionable targets (for others)

▷ Select and use oral and non-verbal language carefully when giving feedback

## Communicating ideas

▷ Create visual impact and use resources and technology to enhance presentations

▷ Analyse audience needs and composition

▷ Appraise practicalities: light, acoustics, availability of equipment, time

▷ Listen to others and address their needs

▷ Use a variety of techniques to organise material and make it engaging and accessible
▷ Summarise without taking notes
▷ Rehearse, evaluate and re-plan

# Learning episodes

## Learning episode 1

**Objective:** to develop knowledge and experience about the different types of roles that can exist within groups.

**Overview:** the starter phase is used by students to get to know another member of the class and to communicate more generally with the other members of the class. The main part of the lesson is used to consider the types of groups and group activities used by teachers at school and to explore the roles needed to be played by individuals within a group, in addition to the subject specific work, to ensure success.

### Suggested resources

■ It is helpful to provide the students with some information about the types of groups that it is possible to work in at school; for example, see Figure 5.1.

### Different Group Types

| | |
|---|---|
| Random | Set ability |
| Friendship | Mixed ability |
| Interest | Learning style |
| Skill | Support |
| Mixed skill | Performance |

**Figure 5.1 Sample list of group types**

- Tables for recording group decisions, responsibilities or discussions may prove helpful; for example, see Figures 5.2 and 5.3.

| Breakdown of what the group has decided to do | Group member in charge of overseeing each area/section | Others involved in each area/section | Deadline for completion of this area |
|---|---|---|---|
|  |  |  |  |
|  |  |  |  |
|  |  |  |  |
|  |  |  |  |

**Figure 5.2  Table for organising group responsibilities**

## Evaluating my group's performance                    My name: ...................................

| Group member | Responsibilities in the classroom | Responsibilities outside the classroom | Overall contribution |
|---|---|---|---|
|  |  |  | Did nothing<br>Did their fair share<br>Did everything |
|  |  |  | Did nothing<br>Did their fair share<br>Did everything |
|  |  |  | Did nothing<br>Did their fair share<br>Did everything |

**Examples of responsibilities:** researching information, making and preparing notes, producing worksheets, producing PowerPoint presentations, developing ideas, creating other resources, photocopying, organising environment (e.g. setting up classroom), leading and managing group.

**Figure 5.3  Table for evaluating my group's performance**

### Detailed description of learning episode 1

#### Starter

1   Ask the class to arrange themselves into pairs and spend a few minutes introducing themselves to each other. Use your judgement to put pairs together to form groups of four. Again, allow a short period of time for introductions.

2   Now use the starter to focus students on the principle that communication is an essential part of working in groups. This can be done by giving students a simple task to complete, but only allowing each member to perform one specific part of the task, thereby forcing students to explain and discuss ideas and actions. The following tasks work well:

   - completing a simple origami exercise
   - making a parachute for a breakable object, such as an egg, from a piece of A4 paper, a 25 cm piece of string and a 15 cm piece of sellotape (scissors are the only additional resource)
   - making a bridge from only paper for a 30 cm gap between two tables that will take the weight of a toy car running across it.

3   After an activity such as one of the tasks above, ask students to discuss their experiences, particularly how the restrictions affected the group-work.

#### Main learning episode

4   Ask the groups to talk about lessons where they work in groups, particularly focusing on the types of groups teachers put them in and the types of class activities teachers use groups for. Take feedback from all the groups.

5   Ask groups to discuss the sheet shown in Figure 5.1 and to decide which types of groups they think would be suitable for different activities. Again, take feedback and ask the groups to explain their choices and thoughts.

6   Introduce the following task to the class:
   *You have been chosen by your headteacher to produce a four-page booklet that is to be given to Year 6 students in nearby primary schools to encourage them to choose your secondary school next year.*

7   Ask groups to discuss the types of jobs that group members will need to do in order to be successful in planning the task, completing it and presenting it to the class.

8   Take feedback, making sure groups refer to timekeeping, leading the group, researching and presenting. Explain that these are all responsibilities that most group-work involves and go into specific detail where necessary or where you feel the students may lack understanding; for example, timekeeping is so often managed by teachers that students are often unskilled in dividing up time and using and managing it effectively.

**9** Give individuals a minute to think about which jobs from the list they think they would be good at and would enjoy doing. Ask groups to share out responsibilities among themselves and for the person taking notes within the group to record who has which responsibility. You may want to have ready-prepared labels for the different responsibilities so that students can easily see which person has which job. Using a table to record the responsibilities can also be helpful.

**10** Ask the groups to begin making the booklet, constantly reminding them of newly decided roles and responsibilities within the group.

### Meta-learning

**1** After the groups have produced at least some of the booklet, encourage them to reflect and evaluate how their group worked together, comparing this experience with other experiences of working in groups in this and/or other subjects.

**2** Invite students to assess their own success in their role.

**3** Alternatively, ask group leaders to assess each individual's success in their areas and then to discuss their assessment with their group members.

**4** Ask students to think of ways they can use any of the explicit work about learning with and from others to help them work more effectively with others in a variety of their subjects.

## Learning episode 2

**Objective:** to gain experience of working with people with different ideas and to learn more effectively because of it.

**Overview:** the starter phase is used to organise the students, initially into pairs with students who share some similarities and then into pairs with other pairs who have some different ideas, feelings and opinions. The main part of the lesson challenges students to work together with similar and dissimilar students to come to a positive outcome for the whole group.

### Suggested resources

■ It is a good idea to have information to stimulate the discussion during the main learning episode. Figure 5.4 is for the activity described in this episode.

ATTITUDES SKILLS KNOWLEDGE

---

## Local Council Budget

You work for your local council and have just received your budget for next year. You have £1,000,000 to spend on 'improving the local area'.

You must decide what is the best way to spend the money in order to most benefit the people who live in the area.

| | |
|---|---|
| Landscaping and 'cleaning up' local park | £50,000 |
| Re-designing and increasing local library | £50,000 |
| Building a new sports and leisure complex | £250,000 |
| Building a water slide centre | £150,000 |
| Building a youth centre for under-16s | £95,000 |
| Running a campaign (bill-board ads, and so on) for decreasing pollution | £50,000 |
| Opening a new shopping mall | £400,000 |
| Marking cycle lanes | £35,000 |
| Security 'CCTV' cameras on every corner | £100,000 |
| Improving local schools' facilities | £250,000 |
| Opening an internet-computer centre | £50,000 |
| Re-designing train station | £250,000 |
| Re-housing the homeless | £100,000 |
| Building a cinema complex | £200,000 |
| Setting up a youth football league club | £80,500 |
| Building a recycling centre | £70,500 |
| Setting up a youth netball league club | £80,500 |
| Creating a tram network to reduce car numbers | £200,000 |

**Figure 5.4  Local council budget sheet**

■ The set of questions in Figure 5.5 is a good resource to use as a meta-learning review of learning episode 2.

- How did your group go about completing the task?
- Were you personally enthusiastic about the task?
- Were there others in your group who felt differently?
- Did different members of your group display different intelligences?
- If so, which seemed to have been more helpful for this type of task?
- If at any point your group found things difficult or that the strategies they were using were not working, what did the group do?
- How did you all support each other?
- Was there a dominant person who made decisions about changes or was a consensus always sought for?
- Did the group make sure that everyone understood how progress was made or did you sometimes have to move on with some people confused or lost?
- Does this matter as long as the group achieved its aim?
- Were you happy with the way your group progressed?
- How did you express your feelings?

**Figure 5.5  Meta-learning review**

## Detailed description of learning episode 2

### Starter

1   Ask students to divide a sheet of A4 paper into four boxes. Tell them to fill the first box with their name and age, the second with their favourite hobby or pastime, the third with a description of something they are really good at and the last with something they do not like (these 'headings' can obviously be changed to other subjects). Ask them to leave the paper open on their table and to move around the room and read as many other people's sheets as possible. Then set them the task of pairing up with someone who is in some way similar to them based on the information on their sheets.

### Main learning episode

2   With the class in their pairs, discuss the advantages and disadvantages of working with people who are similar to you. Record the ideas and opinions put forward by the class. Focusing on the disadvantages of the discussion, ask the class to briefly consider why it might be important to also work with people who are different and have different opinions. Ask each pair to find another pair who expressed some different views, either on their sheets or to a particular subject matter.

3   Explain that each group of four is in role as members in charge of the local council budget for the coming year and hand out the budget sheets (see Figure 5.4). Hand out a title to each member of the group; for example, representing the youth, representing the elderly, representing business, representing parents. This should ensure more debate and give a focus to individual's attempts to negotiate.

4   Ask the groups to consider the task and to conclude why it was important to make sure that there are different opinions represented in each group.

5   Inform the class that they have a certain amount of time to discuss/argue about how the budget should be spent. Stress that they must record their decisions and that they are to present their decisions to the rest of the class afterwards.

6   Remind them of the importance of group members taking responsibility for roles within the group as well as contributing to the task – refer to learning episode 1 as a reminder.

7   Discuss effective negotiation skills, different ways to compromise, the skill of looking at things from different perspectives, voting and any other helpful group strategies that will help students reach a win–win settlement.

8   Give the groups time to complete the task.

9   It is probable that groups will not all agree and they could get stuck in an argument or disagreement about where the money should be spent. You may want to pre-empt this with a discussion before beginning the task or you may decide to focus on it when it arises, or perhaps wait until the end, asking groups to look at the difficulties that arose and whether they managed them well.

10  Allow time in the lesson for groups to give feedback and for a general discussion to take place.

### Meta-learning

Wherever you choose to end the activity, the meta-cognitive review resource (Figure 5.5) works as a useful review of how students' feel about learning with and from others.

## Transferring the skill and knowledge

In PE or design and technology: set students the task of working with everyone in the class by the end of the year and ask them to keep a record of who they worked with, in what type of group and for what type of activity.

# Progression statement

When planning learning-to-learn, you will want to build progression into your schemes of learning and learning plans. In this section, we have described progression as we see it and hope this will help you map out learning-to-learn as a continuous part of your curriculum.

| Communicating ideas | I organise the content of my presentation to make it more effective and engaging. I can use overhead projection, flashcards, posters, handouts and PowerPoint. I use a variety of engaging styles when presenting material and always rehearse before I present. I am confident presenting orally in front of large groups and take into account body language, tone of voice and eye contact. |
| --- | --- |
| Assessing and making progress | I accept constructive feedback from others and try to use it to improve my learning. I ensure that I have a full grasp of any material or information before teaching it. I check the understanding of those I am teaching and respond accordingly. I make sure that all the contributions by others are respected and considered. I can use a mark scheme to mark my own work and that of others, including formative comment. I am careful to discuss the work and not the person when assessing the work of peers. I assess my learning as I go along honestly and against the learning objectives including creating my own mark schemes. I can provide evidence to support the assessments I have made. |
| Understanding group dynamics and managing relationships | I am happy to work in different groups and with different people and I can choose the best type of group for a particular task. I can explain the pros and cons of different types of groups. I can explain the different roles needed for a group and I can decide which roles are appropriate for which task. I can make decisions and plans with others and accept my share of responsibility for managing the difficulties that we encounter. I know how to work towards consensus. |

*As students develop into established learners, their increased understanding and awareness will be reflected as follows.*

| Communicating ideas | I can present to a whole class. I am aware of the audience I am presenting to. I know that there are different ways to present. I use ICT to help prepare my resources. | I have presented to small groups in my classes. I use visual aids. I use reprographic equipment. I use various forms of ICT. |
| --- | --- | --- |
| Assessing and making progress | I can give constructive feedback to others. I support others with praise and help when required. I make sure that I understand the targets my teachers set and try to achieve them. | I understand what is meant by formative and summative assessment. I sometimes assess my own learning and that of my classmates in all my subjects. |
| Understanding group dynamics and managing relationships | I am happy to work with others when I am asked by the teacher and I try to do my fair share and take a leading role within groups. I know there are different types of groups that can be used for different tasks and the different roles that people have in groups. I understand the importance of following instructions when working in a group and meeting group deadlines. | |

*Initially, students may connect to the learning in the following ways.*

## What the teachers say

'Teachers tend to use peer teaching quite a lot, so if some kids have a particular problem, instead of bringing them all round a desk and giving a demonstration, where you'll still lose some of them no matter how good you are, it is quite a good idea to pick one child out. It is an even better idea to pick one kid out who is perhaps not high ability and show them a particular skill or, I call it "Eureka", a particular concept that you know the others are going to have to have at some later stage and use that student as a peer teacher.

So you can say to another student, "You've got that problem, why don't you go and see Jaswinder. He knows how to help you solve that problem. He can explain it." So he becomes a sort of expert at that. There's a real modelling of kids as experts. I quite quickly get kids to do little demonstrations to two or three others. So that kind of learning from each other is the formal bit that you would use a lot of. When the student in role as expert is delivering a demonstration to other kids, or talking to other kids about that skill in technology, we take some time to help them develop the skills that they need to communicate their ideas and their thinking.

For example, I'm thinking about one kid in Year 11, who I'm teaching at the moment, who's a real expert on a bit of software that I taught to him after school at one of the clubs. I made him aware that he was going to have to demonstrate the skill to other people and I tried to talk him through the types of things he'd have to do when he was teaching other students and also the types of misunderstandings they were going to have. I very much brought him into the teacher world in this instance and I certainly do it to let students know that when teaching others they must let them make mistakes before they correct it. And that's definitely a skill that students can take to other subject areas, although I often in the past haven't highlighted that enough.

And then there's the more typical kind of group-work – students working in pairs and threes, which happens a lot at Key Stage 3, although in technology they usually have specific jobs to do. It is not often where you'd have a group working where they would have a project to do. It would be much more along the lines of batch production, for example, where it is "You do this bit, that's your role." Or you might put them together and say, "Right, you're going to have to produce this so put yourself together into a production team."

Part of the technology task will also be to work out who plays what role within the group and they work that out beforehand. In fact, part of the marks will be allocated to how well they break down the task, including things like, "Whose going to organise things?" and "Whose going to provide quality assurance?" We find that they work quite well together and perhaps that's because there's a real reason for working together, which perhaps there isn't in some other subjects. I don't call it group activities, I call it working in teams and I use that term "teams" because it has a connotation to me that you have a part to play in a team. If you're not there, the team can't function; whereas a group to me could function without that one person not being there somehow or other. So if you take the screen printing exercise. It is very difficult to do it on your own so working in a team is the only realistic way of being able to produce the work. The result of that is that if somebody does not do their role properly, the outcome is going to be very obviously poor at the end and it is usually quite easy to spot which area within the team didn't work very well or why it didn't work very well. Sitting down for an hour beforehand and working out the flow diagram of who's going to do what, isn't unusual. I am constantly trying to model the real world, which brings in negotiation skills, leadership skills, learning to listen. I might talk about those in the context of getting them to work more effectively. Quite often I will stop teams in conflict, over colours or designs or something, all of which they feel quite strongly about and discuss the merits of both sides and the pros and cons of producing both prototypes or reaching a compromise and just producing one. This demonstrates the importance of sharing lots of ideas and also is realistic of the real world, which I'm always trying to model. So in the real world you would have two "mock ups" and you'd test them to see which the best one is.'

*Dave Curran*, design and technology teacher

## Taking it further

Try to vary the types and sizes of different groups as often as possible, ensuring that opportunities for reflection and discussion about the groups are built into starters and plenaries.

Make sure that students are always aware of the different roles they are playing within the group, as well the subject-specific focus of the group-work. They could perhaps keep a record of the different roles they play across a period of time, either in one subject or across many.

Using the knowledge developed in the previous skill, 'Understanding self as a learner', build in opportunities for students to share their knowledge about learning and assessment with one another.

When a class is involved in any group activity, show them Figure 5.1 and ask them to decide which type of group they are in. You could let them keep a record of the group types and set them the task of keeping a record of the different types of groups they are part of at other times; in lessons, at recess, in sport, and so on.

Ask students to try to use what they have learned about group-work in other classes and to keep a record of whether it has helped them work more effectively with others.

Discuss fictitious examples of group scenarios and ask the students to discuss the areas of collaborative learning that seem successful and those that do not – two examples are given below.

●●●●●●●●●●●●●●●●●●●●●●●●●●●●●●●●●●●●●●●●●●●●●●●●●●●●●●●●●●●●●●●●●

Ravi is a student in a Year 9 mixed ability maths class. He is friendly with a group of five boys in the class and all six of them find maths difficult and are working at Level 4. They have been finding the work quite difficult recently and have stopped working hard in some of the lessons.

There are six other boys in the class – three are working at Level 5 and three at Level 6. There are also 14 girls in the class – one with a Level 8, four with Level 7, five with Level 6, two with Level 5 and two with Level 4.

The teacher has decided that the class are going to work in groups of three to five for the next three weeks. The groups are going to be given a number of different maths tasks to solve together to help them develop their maths skills.

*Who should Ravi work with in his group?*

●●●●●●●●●●●●●●●●●●●●●●●●●●●●●●●●●●●●●●●●●●●●●●●●●●●●●●●●●●●●●●●●●

Ilhan is a student in a middle set in English. She enjoys discussions and drama work and so do her five friends, who are also in the class. Two of her friends are good at writing and there are five boys and five other girls who are also good at all areas in English (reading, writing and speaking and listening).

There are three other boys and five other girls who are excellent at reading and writing, but do not get involved in discussions and do not enjoy the drama activities.

They have recently been studying the news.

The teacher has set the class the task of getting into a group of four and over the next three weeks they have to plan, research and produce a newspaper and a television news show. The newspaper should be at least ten pages of A3 and the news show should be a ten-minute performance.

*Who should Ilhan work with in her group?*

●●●●●●●●●●●●●●●●●●●●●●●●●●●●●●●●●●●●●●●●●●●●●●●●●●●●●●●●●●●●●●●●●

It is important to encourage students to vary the groups they work in and to think about the make up of the group and how effective they are in their shared strengths and weaknesses. Asking students to assess themselves in key areas relating to the objectives of what they are trying to achieve and then sharing this information with others to form suitable groups can help with this. For example, ask students to give themselves a score between 0 and 100 in the following areas: creativity, never giving up, leadership, listening to others. Then ask the class to share the information and form balanced, mixed-ability groups in these areas.

# 6 Planning

'Gift, like genius, I often think only means an infinite capacity for taking pains.'

JANE ELLICE HOPKINS

## Introduction

The skill of planning is beneficial in almost all aspects of everyday life. People are constantly planning – their shopping, evening out, a children's party, next holiday, family, career, finances and so on. Being able to plan effectively is a life skill that makes a real difference to the experience and quality of life and to feelings of being in control, and hence of wellbeing.

Within the school curriculum, planning comes into every subject, both as a requirement for learning certain components of a subject and as a recurrent theme of effective learning. For example, learning how to plan investigations is part of the science curriculum; planning essays is part of the English and history curriculum; story boarding part of the art and media curriculum; planning 'research' and 'making' is fundamental in technology subjects. In addition, students are expected to be able to plan their learning, from very simple tasks such as planning what to bring to school every day or how to lay out a page in their exercise book, to how to approach a task set by the teacher in class or planning their time at home to complete homework, coursework and revision. Our experience as teachers is that those students who plan effectively are the ones that achieve well. When a parent tells you how his son in Year 11 has planned out all his time for the next month to get his revision and coursework completed, you just know that he will produce good grades in his exams.

Is planning taught explicitly in your school, in your subject? Can students describe how to plan effectively? Do they plan effectively? Would it help if they could? Planning is quite a complex skill and involves more than working through a series of steps. Even when students know about how to plan, they do not always do so. Why is this? Is it because there is an emotional component involved as well? We suspect it is connected with two of the attitudes that we have described: resilience and resourcefulness.

In the 1980s, the Assessment of Performance Unit carried out research into students' approaches to planning scientific investigations, which is described in *Assessment Matters: No. 6 Planning and Carrying Out Investigations* (Strang et al. 1991). Their work showed that it is very difficult for students to plan experiments from start to finish without any opportunity to do the experiment. It also showed that students needed a mental model of both the investigation and the concepts under investigation. There are two important messages here: developing good planning skills is best achieved through an iterative process of planning, doing, reflecting and revising planning; and the success of planning is inseparable from the subject-specific concepts under consideration.

'Sir, what is the secret of your success?'
'Two words.'
'And, sir, what are they?'
'Right decisions.'
'And how do you make right decisions?'
'One word.'
'And, what is that?'
'Experience.'
'And how do you get experience?'
'Two words'
'And, sir, what are they?'
'Wrong decisions.'

## Attitude development

| | |
|---|---|
| Resourcefulness | ✓ ✓ ✓ ✓ |
| Resilience | ✓ ✓ ✓ |
| Responsiveness | ✓ ✓ ✓ ✓ |
| Reciprocity | ✓ ✓ ✓ |
| Reflectiveness | ✓ ✓ ✓ ✓ |

# Skills and knowledge breakdown

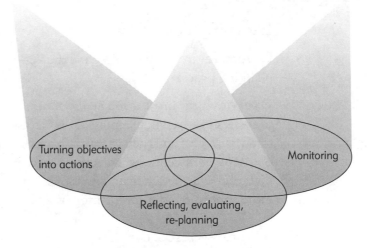

## Turning objectives into actions

▷ Turn objectives into end product – 'imagine the end'
▷ Break overall task down into smaller steps
▷ Identify any background research needed
▷ Take advice
▷ Prioritise tasks
▷ Prepare action plan with timescales and deadlines
▷ Carry out risk assessments
▷ Create a vision of yourself being successful
▷ Expect to discover unforeseen challenges as plan is carried out
▷ Plan a reward for sticking to the final deadline

## Monitoring

▷ Check progress against action plan regularly
▷ Check progress against objectives and assessment criteria regularly
▷ Check timescales and deadlines regularly
▷ Make wall charts, calendars, tick lists
▷ Make mini-deadlines
▷ Plan rewards for achieving small steps
▷ Manage distractions and do the worst first
▷ Adjust lifestyle to get the job done
▷ Plan for breaks and leisure and for the unexpected

## Reflecting, evaluating, re-planning

▷ Review plan against objectives
▷ Adjust plan as necessary
▷ Review strategies used
▷ Note lessons learned and set targets for next time
▷ Re-plan as necessary

# Learning episodes

## Learning episode 1

**Objective:** to be able to describe the key components of a simple planning process.

**Overview:** the first learning episode aims to teach the students the basic processes involved in planning. It uses an easy example to get the students to devise a plan and then to reflect back on the processes involved. The outcome of this episode is a general description of the planning process that can be applied in many situations and developed further to create more sophisticated planning processes for specific subjects.

### Suggested resources

- CD/tape/MP3 of Lennon's song 'Imagine'
- mini whiteboards
- A1 paper
- recorded 'mystery sounds, pictures and objects'
- blank cards

### Detailed description of learning episode 1

#### Starter

1   To plan well it is important to use imagination and to picture the end result, so using imagination is a key component to introduce in learning episode 1. One way to achieve this is by playing a short extract from the song 'Imagine' by John Lennon and asking the students to write on mini whiteboards any words that have the same meaning as ' imagine'.

2   Follow this by asking the students to use their imagination to work something out. Try one or more of the following examples: play a number of different sounds to the class (keys rattling, garage door closing) and ask the students what they think these sounds are; use the spotlight tool on an interactive whiteboard to show a tiny part of a picture; hold up a shape revealing only the tip of the shape and ask the students to work out what it is; or ask the students to feel something in a bag and to determine what it is.

3   Conclude with a brief class discussion about how they have used their imagination to come up with ideas.

#### Main learning episode

4   Introduce the objective of teaching the students how to plan effectively.

5   Talk about what is meant by planning, when we plan and why we plan. Invite the students to give examples of when they have used planning.

6   Now ask them to plan an activity with which they are very familiar in order to establish some of the components of 'The Planning Cycle'; for example, an end-of-term party for the class, a trip or a charity activity.

7 Ask the students to start by describing in detail what the event will be like. Encourage them to imagine the end result.

8 Having established a detailed description of the party (or similar), the students should think about all the steps they would need to take to prepare for the party. They could fill in a table with four columns ('Task', 'When', 'Who', 'How long'), or complete blank cards for each of the tasks and then arrange them in order, or fill blanks on a flow diagram.

## Meta-learning

1 The next step is to establish the common themes in devising a plan. At this point, the students should reflect on the process they have been using in order to devise an outline of the planning process.

2 You could conclude with a class discussion about whether the order of the processes matters and how much flexibility there is in the way they approach planning.

3 Ask the students to create a summary of the key steps to successful planning that can be referred to later. An idea adopted at Villiers was to create a small card to use as a prompt for lessons in all subjects.

# Learning episode 2

**Objective:** to be able to identify important subject-specific features to add to a general planning process to tailor it for different subjects.

**Overview:** learning episode 2 gives the students the opportunity to apply the planning cycle they devised in the previous learning episode to a specific task within a particular subject. The example lesson is science but any subject could be used. The aim is to give the students the opportunity to use and test out their planning process, to recognise that plans can change as they are put into practice and to reflect on the significance of this. Finally, the aim will be to continue to make the planning cycle more sophisticated by including subject-specific components.

## Suggested resources

- thermometers
- ice
- salt
- beakers
- stopclocks
- scales
- access to internet
- textbooks.

## Detailed description of learning episode 2

### Starter

1 Recap the key steps to successful planning. For example, put some of the steps on the board and ask students to recall the missing steps and then put all the steps in the correct (a workable) order.

### Main learning episode

2   Set a subject-specific planning task for the class. For example, plan an investigation to answer the following question: 'Why is salt used to melt ice on roads in winter'. Choose an example to fit in with the scheme of learning or invite the students to devise a question for investigation related to something topical.

3   Pose the question to the class, explore their ideas and recall the first step they will perform in planning their investigation.

4   Show them the available equipment to act as a cue for their plan and ask them to start on their plans, emphasising the need to begin at the end. Refer them to the key steps for successful planning.

5   When they are ready, they should be allowed to complete their investigation without much comment from you about their plan. This will come later.

6   When they have completed their investigation, ask the students to compare what they did with their initial plan. This could be done by completing a table of similarities and differences or they could annotate their original plan with coloured pen to show the changes they have made.

### Meta-learning

1   When the task is completed, discuss with the class the differences between planning the investigation and doing the investigation and what they have learned about planning, in science, in particular.

2   Discuss how the students managed their time. Did they estimate how long different tasks would take? Did they monitor time? How did they do this? This would be a good opportunity to introduce the idea of reflecting, evaluating and re-planning as a key component of the planning process. Try bringing in some specific techniques for managing time.

3   Finish by looking back at the planning process the students devised in the previous learning episode and add to it. Try putting together a planning toolkit with the class.

4   Undoubtedly, there will be other subject-specific aspects that will need further attention. In science, these might include the number of readings taken, the use of controls, or the number of times the experiment is repeated. These can be introduced in later learning episodes to continue the development of more sophisticated subject-specific planning.

## Transferring the skill and knowledge

- In English and history: to help students learn to plan essays.
- In art: to help students plan their response to a stimulus.
- In PE: to help teams plan a winning strategy.
- In geography and history: to help plan fieldwork projects.

# Progression statement

When planning learning-to-learn, you will want to build progression into your schemes of learning and learning plans. In this section, we have described progression as we see it and hope this will help you map out learning-to-learn as a continuous part of your curriculum.

| | |
|---|---|
| **Reflecting, evaluating, re-planning** | I am able to evaluate the strengths and weaknesses of my plan as I go along and when I have completed my task, and can re-plan based on my evaluation. My evaluation takes account of what is important in each specific subject. I can evaluate the strategies I used, including time management, to carry out my plans and summarise lessons learned for next time. I can distinguish between the planning skills I have learned and the learning attitudes needed to complete a successful plan. I can summarise new subject-specific learning established through carrying out my plan and separate it from my learning about the planning process. |
| **Monitoring** | I use a variety of techniques to help me manage time. I keep a critical eye as I carry out my plan, checking back to the original objective. I check my progress against my plan on a regular basis and make adjustments as necessary. I learn new techniques, as I go along, if I need to. I change my plans when I get new insights as I carry out the task. I check timescales and deadlines regularly, and am able to manage distractions. |
| **Turning objectives into actions** | I can use subject knowledge to turn objectives into actions and can carry out background research to help me plan effectively. I know how to seek advice as part of the research phase of my planning. I know how to plan in different subjects and what is important for different subjects. I can take part in an informed discussion with my peers to explore concepts before we begin planning. I can turn broad 'open' tasks into a series of specific and clear objectives and prepare plans for these. I can prepare an action plan with timescales and deadlines. I can carry out risk assessments for my plans and expect to meet unforeseen challenges as I carry out my plan. |

*As students develop into established learners, their increased understanding and awareness will be reflected as follows.*

| | | |
|---|---|---|
| **Reflecting, evaluating, re-planning** | I can compare what I did with my original plan and use this to improve my plans. | |
| **Monitoring** | I can use my plan to guide me. | I can use time-management techniques to help me complete my tasks. |
| **Turning objectives into actions** | I know how to plan. I can work out the steps I need to take to carry out a simple task. I can put the tasks in the right order. I can plan with a group of my peers to divide the tasks between us. I work out a plan before starting to do a task. | I have used planning in a number of different subjects. I know that planning helps my work. I know it is important to use my plans when doing tasks. I know that meeting deadlines is important if tasks are to be completed. |

*Initially, students may connect to the learning in the following ways.*

# What the teachers say

The head of art at Villiers made the following points about planning in art.

## Drawing and planning

'The students do a series of quick drawings; they evaluate the parts of the drawing that work and the other parts that they want to change. They continue by developing the ideas they like, drafting and redrafting, changing things like the scale and the position. They do this by going through a process of trial and error before they work up their final drawings. The biggest challenge is getting the students to develop their ideas. They tend to want to stick to the first idea they come up with.'

## Photography and planning

'In a photography lesson, we might give the students a title like "viewpoints". They explore the idea by brainstorming and taking some photographs. They draw a basic storyboard, take some photographs and then they revisit the storyboard with their initial photographs to start planning out their film. For example, they will plan the low-down shots, and the close ups, to produce their draft storyboard. After this they take more photographs. When they are editing the photographs they are developing plans again.

In fact the marking component in their exam is called "planning".

Planning in art involves making a response to a stimulus and ideas generation. Planning in art is all about the creative process and using imagination. We find it a challenge to get all our students to engage fully in this process. The main struggle is to encourage the students to think through their plans before starting their practical work and to persuade them to explore and develop a range of ideas. Recently, we have started to use more of an iterative process in planning, so that the students plan, do, plan again and so on and this seems to be working, especially with the boys.'

## Resources

| Task | Estimated time for task | Actual time for task |
|------|-------------------------|----------------------|
|      |                         |                      |
|      |                         |                      |
|      |                         |                      |
|      |                         |                      |

**Figure 6.1  Resources for planning**

## Taking it further

Focus on particular aspects of planning; for example, by giving students a clock face and asking them to estimate the length of time tasks will take. Students should then complete a table with estimated and actual times and use this as a means of focusing on time management (see Figure 6.1). Introduce timers (watches) for students to set in order to give themselves timed warnings. Introduce the notion of allocating one student as timekeeper. Review the success of timekeeping strategies at the end.

Look at the area of reliability to help students understand the importance of repetition in science experiments. For example:

■ Toss a coin and look at the number of heads and number of tails depending on number of throws.
■ Test to see whether students can tell the difference between different brands of the same fizzy drink.
■ Use invented and published statistics to lead a discussion on a controversial issue, such as 'All teenagers are lazy'. Use this to explore the notion of the reliability of statistics.

Give the students longer open projects to plan. Introduce mini-deadlines along the way; for example, presenting some initial findings and inviting questions for consideration, or preparing a budget plan and bidding for funds. Ask the students to put key milestones into their plans. Introduce students to project planning software.

Invite artists or writers or business people to talk to students about the processes they go through to plan and develop their work.

Develop techniques with the drama department to help students visualise a successful process and outcomes.

Review students work after plans and tasks are completed. Explore the need for resourcefulness in the development of plans. Compare examples where the students have investigated a range of resources with those where students have done limited research.

# 7 Investigating resources

*'Our progress as a nation can be no swifter than our progress in education. The human mind is our fundamental resource.'*

JOHN F. KENNEDY

## Introduction

Every day we absorb an enormous amount of information from a wide variety of sources. Some of this we act on or react to, some we think about and internalise and some we just notice. Our memory clearly plays a part in our ability to process information as does our state of mind at the time.

In 1956, George Miller presented two key ideas about memory and a person's ability to process information, which are directly relevant to this area of ASK. First, he stated that seven was somehow a 'magic' number because the short-term memory can only hold between five and nine chunks of information (seven plus or minus two). A 'chunk' is any meaningful unit: possibly words, digits, positions on a chess board or people's faces. The concept of 'chunking' (see Chapter 8) became a basic element of subsequent theories of memory. The second concept uses the computer as a model for human learning. Like a computer, the brain takes in information, processes it to change its form and content, stores and locates it and creates responses to it. Thus, investigating resources and information processing involve collecting and representing information (encoding), storing the information (retention) and recalling the information when needed (retrieval). For these reasons we can see that investigating resources and the subsequent processing of information are intrinsically linked to developing memory in ASK.

Traditionally, investigating resources in the secondary school curriculum involved being told by the teacher which pages of a given textbook to read or, at best, a session in the school library in which learners may have been given more freedom to explore books of their own choice. Clearly in the 'Information Age' this approach is no longer sufficient. Before we present the ASK breakdown of investigating resources, consider your answers to the following questions:

- Which resources do your students regularly have access to for the purposes of enhancing their learning?
- Does the range of resources reflect those that your students are likely to use in adult life?

- Are you making full and appropriate use of ICT and resources such as the internet?
- Are students given the opportunity to use resources that suit their particular needs or personal preferences?
- Are students able to sift through too much information and extract just the key points or relevant information?
- Are students explicitly taught different ways of re-formatting information, such as note-making, to help them remember and recall it?

## Attitude development

| | |
|---|---|
| Resourcefulness | ✓ ✓ ✓ ✓ |
| Resilience | ✓ |
| Responsiveness | ✓ ✓ |
| Reciprocity | ✓ ✓ ✓ |
| Reflectiveness | ✓ ✓ ✓ |

# Skills and knowledge breakdown

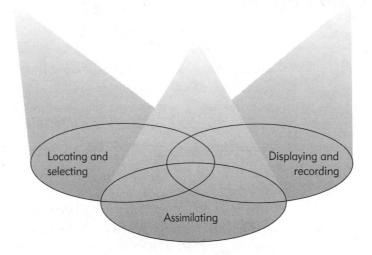

## Locating and selecting

▷ Get a quick and accurate impression of your resource using skimming and scanning, indices, contents, blurb, site maps and so on
▷ Apply assessment criteria/learning objectives/research questions to the prospective resources
▷ Make judgements about the usefulness of a resource
▷ Use contents lists, indices and site maps to locate information within a resource
▷ Use experts (including teachers) for guidance
▷ Use the internet as a source of information
▷ Use libraries as a source of information

## Displaying and recording

▷ Learn different ways to set out notes
▷ Identify keywords, information and ideas
▷ Form own phrases to include keywords and ideas
▷ Recognise hierarchies of information
▷ Select best note-making method given the purpose of the notes and learner's own style

## Assimilating

▷ Summarise without taking notes
▷ Detect bias
▷ Assess, once it has been used, the usefulness of a resource against the learning outcomes

# Learning episodes

## Learning episode 1

**Objective:** to learn and use different techniques for displaying and recording information gained from investigating a resource (including note-taking, identifying key points/keywords and choosing a note-making method to suit the task and personal preference).

**Overview:** the starter uses a whole-class brainstorm or small groups with feedback to help students discover how they will find all the information they will need for completing the task. A whole-class question-and-answer session should lead to a shared understanding of various note-making techniques, such as prose, bullet points, mind maps. The main learning episode uses a group activity where students rotate in a 'carousel' to find out as much information as possible from each other in a short time. In a paired activity, students present findings on the original topic to the rest of the group via a poster.

### Suggested resources

- Visual stimuli around topic to be investigated, such as newspaper articles, magazines, pictures from internet.
- Flipchart/whiteboard to record results of brainstorm
- Cards/worksheets containing information about chosen topic – these could be printed off from the internet
- Sugar paper, coloured pens, glue, scissors and so on for producing poster/display

### Detailed description of learning episode 1

#### Starter

1   Either as whole-class brainstorm or in groups of three or four on tables with feedback, students consider the following task:
    *Imagine you are a newspaper reporter. Your boss has directed you to write an article about a scientific discovery (about our solar system) made at a local university but you know nothing about it. Where will you go to find out, and how will you find all the information you need?*
2   Key questions to encourage students to think about possible resources to investigate are:
    - What are the advantages/disadvantages of using people as a source of information compared to books, newspapers or the internet?
    - What are the advantages and disadvantages of using the internet as a source of information? (Note: this question will get students to think about 'too much information' and the need to select only what is relevant for the task in hand. This idea will be developed

more fully in learning episode 2. Provide a table for students in which they can record their thoughts.)

■ What are the advantages and disadvantages of using as wide a range of information sources as possible? (Note: this question is designed to lead students towards the need for informed, balanced and unbiased information. The concept of bias should be addressed and developed through subsequent learning episodes.)

## Main learning episode

**3**  Instigate a whole-class question-and-answer session using the following: 'What different ways are there of making notes?' (Note: you may wish to have explored this more fully in a previous lesson or learning episode.) Record students' answers on the whiteboard.

**4**  Display examples of prose, bullet points, flow-charts, spider diagrams and mind maps using a projector and screen or an interactive whiteboard.

**5**  If time is available, discuss pros, cons and appropriate situations in which to use each type or style.

**6**  As a group activity, divide the class into four equal-sized groups. Two of the groups are each given a card/sheet of paper that show a different piece of information about the scientific discovery. Some information could be relevant/irrelevant or in a variety of formats depending on the group of students.

**7**  These two groups stand in a separate circle in any space in the classroom with the other two groups each standing around them forming concentric circles. Every member of the outer circle asks their partner in the inner circle questions about the information they have and records the information using their chosen note-making techniques from the previous phase. They have one minute only to do this before the teacher signals to the class that they are to rotate to the next person and repeat the same process.

**8**  This continues six or seven times until every student in the outer circle has seen every member of the corresponding inner circle.

**9**  Direct all members of either outer circle to form a pair with any member of either inner circle. They are to work together using the information gained from the previous activity to produce a poster informing people about the solar system/scientific discovery.

**10**  Pairs explain/present their posters to the rest of the class.

## Meta-learning

■ As a whole class, discuss the following questions:
■ How easy did you find it to record all the information in such a short time?
■ What note-making techniques did you use?

- Did your chosen note-making style make it more easy/difficult to record the information quickly?

- How easy was it to use your notes to extract the key information needed to produce the poster?

- If you had known in advance that you would be asked to produce a poster, would you have made your notes differently?

- When do you think you will next have to make notes to record information quickly? How will you use what you have learned today?

## Learning episode 2

**Objective:** to select and re-format only the relevant information from a variety of different information sources to complete a variety of tasks.

**Overview:** the starter phase recaps the key learning from episode 1. A whole-class discussion looks at ways in which information can be processed or re-formatted. The main learning episode uses a group activity where students select, process and re-format information on a particular topic according to purpose/audience. Groups then pair up to compare/contrast different approaches.

### Suggested resources

Information from a variety of different sources and in a variety of different formats on chosen topic. Some examples might include books, worksheets, magazines, scientific journals, CD-ROM, internet, DVD.

### Detailed description of learning episode 2

#### Starter

1 As a whole class, recap the key learning points from episode 1.
2 Discuss different ways that information from various sources can be 'processed' or re-formatted: diagrams, pictures, graphs, charts, bullet points, spider diagrams, mind maps, audio files and so on. Examples can be shown; for example, using data projector/interactive whiteboard.
3 Discuss the following question: 'In which careers/professions would people most need to use the skills of interrogating resources and selecting/reformatting information?'

#### Main learning episode

4 Divide the class into six groups. The groups can be seated together around a central resource table.
5 Information should be provided about a topic, such as 'Life on a tropical island', that can address many different areas of the curriculum

as illustrated in the individual group tasks below. (According to available classroom space, time and other resources, the information could be on cards/worksheets, books, magazines, CD–ROM, internet, audio, video and so on.)

**6** a) Two of the groups should be given the task of producing a passage of descriptive writing about the island (English).

b) Two of the groups are required to produce a scale map of the island showing its key features (geography and maths).

c) Two of the groups are to design and draw (artist's impression, diagrams) a marina complex for the new harbour development on the island that must incorporate certain features; for example, shops, restaurants, sports facilities (design and technology, graphics, art).

**7** Each pair of groups who have worked on the same task should join together to compare and contrast what they have produced and how.

**8** A nominated spokesperson from each group rotates around all the other groups to share how the group selected which information to include and how they decided to reformat and present it.

### Meta-learning

**1** Pairs of groups from the previous phase consider some or all the following questions:
- How did you decide which information to use for your task?
- How could you tell quickly whether or not a particular piece of information was going to be useful or not?
- How did you record the relevant key points to help you complete your task?

**2** Pairs should give feedback to the rest of the class about their thoughts to the above questions and discuss where else they may use these skills, that is, transferability to other subject areas and applications outside the school environment.

## Transferring the skill and knowledge

In history: students could be presented with a range of secondary resources and asked to produce either a biased or unbiased summary for presentation about a key historical event.

In science: internet-based research project. Students research a controversial current scientific issue – for example, human embryo cloning, cosmetic surgery – and prepare for a debate. Different groups of students have to present an argument either for or against the issue and give reasons to back up their judgements.

# Progression statement

When planning learning-to-learn, you will want to build progression into your schemes of learning and learning plans. In this section, we have described progression as we see it and hope this will help you map out learning-to-learn as a continuous part of your curriculum.

| | | |
|---|---|---|
| **Assimilating** | I regularly put text into my own words to aid my understanding.<br>I can summarise information in my own words in a variety of appropriate forms, without making notes.<br>I can identify the type and extent of bias within a source. | |
| **Displaying and recording** | I can pick out the keywords in a text for a specific task or purpose.<br>I can skim read to get an overview.<br>I can scan information for meaning.<br>I skim and scan regularly and effectively.<br>I gather and synthesise information from a range of texts.<br>I know some of the different ways to make notes.<br>I have a range of ways to set out information.<br>I try to use an appropriate method of making notes.<br>I take notes as a natural part of my learning. | I can select the most effective way of taking notes from a particular source for a particular task.<br>I recognise hierarchies of information in my note-making.<br>I highlight the most important points from texts.<br>I understand that annotation is an important method of immediately recording my thinking.<br>I use annotation to record my initial response to sources before any shared study.<br>I use annotation to develop my questioning skills. |
| **Locating and selecting** | I can choose appropriate ways of getting information for different tasks and purposes.<br>I can gather information from appropriate places outside the school as well as within.<br>I am creative in my approach to finding resources.<br>I am always looking for new ways to find information. | |

*As students develop into established learners, their increased understanding and awareness will be reflected as follows.*

| | | |
|---|---|---|
| **Assimilating** | I can decide whether or not a particular resource was useful for a particular task and use this to my advantage for future learning.<br>I can summarise the key points of a particular resource by taking notes in a suitable format.<br>I have a basic understanding of what is meant by bias. | |
| **Displaying and recording** | I read for understanding.<br>I look for the keywords in a text.<br>I am careful and accurate in copying information from texts. | I can pick the appropriate text to copy that is linked to or explains keywords.<br>I know what is meant by annotation. |
| **Locating and selecting** | I usually ask my teacher if I need to find out some information.<br>I know that the library is another good place to go to find things out and sometimes ask the librarian to find me a helpful book.<br>I have some idea of how the internet can be used to help locate resources. | |

*Initially, students may connect to the learning in the following ways..*

## What the teachers say

'Students are taught at the start of their journey in English at Villiers the importance of investigating resources in order to enhance their learning. They are taught to locate and select, display and record, and assimilate resources.

For locating and selecting, they are guided to think about: the appropriate resources available and their location (be they in the library, on the internet, at theatres, at cinemas, in newspapers, in magazines, in museums, to name but a few); the ability to skim and scan texts in order to make judgements; the use of their teacher as a resource and other adults who are specialists in the area being studied.

For displaying and recording, they are guided to think about the various note-making techniques available and the ability to identify keywords, ideas about the relevant multi-modal texts used in English.

Assimilating is yet another important strand to investigating resources in English as it allows students to assess their notes for relevance, summarise, show awareness of the source of the resource, as well as making them user friendly for their own personal learning styles.

Investigating resources in English is a road our students embark upon at Villiers almost every lesson, a journey that with each new step strengthens their previous understanding and learning.

*Amanda Sara*, English teacher

## Taking it further

Having completed the two learning episodes, future work to develop students' skills in this area might involve the use of note-making and presentation styles that not only suit a student's personal preference but also the context of the information being investigated. At a still more sophisticated level, the students might be challenged to present re-formatted information in a style that suits the intended audience.

Classroom activities involving the interrogation of text, or internet-based information sources, followed by the re-formatting and presentation in one or more of the following contexts might help to develop this skill, providing that the teacher structures appropriate opportunities for a meta-learning review (see Chapter 3 for more detail on this):

- A classroom poster for Year 6 students
- A presentation to their year group as part of an assembly
- A newspaper article or press release
- A debate
- A courtroom trial
- An article on the evening news specifically targeted at young people.

Other follow-up learning episodes might focus on developing the use of annotation of a text-based resource to develop questioning skills to enable students to deeply interrogate a given resource. The technique of 'hot-seating' where the teacher role-plays an expert in the particular field, a famous scientist or historical figure might provide an effective and entertaining means of allowing the students to trial their questions arising from annotating the text and to see if they are effective in investigating the resource more fully.

Having taught the students how to identify the type and extent of inherent bias associated with a particular resource, a higher-order task could encourage the students to deliberately introduce bias into their re-formatting and presentation to make their information more appealing to the intended audience. Although this activity may not be appropriate for all students, it provides an entertaining and valuable learning experience whose scope is limited only by the imagination (and perhaps courage) of the teacher.

# Developing memory

*'What did we do last lesson?'*
*'I don't know.'*
*'What do you mean, you don't know?'*
*'I mean, I can't remember.'*

## Introduction

Memory is at the heart of who we are and what we think. Watching Guy Pearce's character in the film *Momento*, clearly illustrates the impossibility of basic existence without memory, as he struggles to cope with life's challenges. Without having a memory to rely on, he resorts to tattoos and endless note-taking to help him make sense of his existence.

Making any sort of progress in absolutely anything requires at the very least recall of memory of some sort. Luckily for the vast majority of us, our brain takes care of most of the business of remembering what we need to know. We can recall at will the essential information of daily life: names, dates, locations, functions and so on. There is an instinctual, biological side to memory that means, on the whole, we can take it for granted. But by doing this, as with most things we take for granted, we neglect to learn about how memory works and never master its potential. Our memories are closely linked to our emotions and they are not perfect. The way we remember an event may be entirely different to the way someone else remembers it. This is even more likely if we are personally involved in the event or have a vested interest. In addition to this, our memory can fail us entirely. You know that sudden surprise when you cannot recall something – a pin number, someone's name, what you're supposed to be doing or where you put something. Memory failure can be a powerful reminder of just how important it is to keep our memory functioning reliably.

### Memory in schools

Traditionally, the ability to memorise well has always been considered an essential part of successful study. This is because of the large amounts of information that students need to retain and then recall; from memorising new vocabulary in languages, through formulas in mathematics, to names and dates in history, memory has always been at the heart of what is done in schools. Exams have historically been as much about recalling stored information as they have about applying knowledge and learning. And yet how often do teachers explicitly teach their students useful knowledge and theory about how memory works or give students opportunities to develop appropriate strategies to use for different tasks? Perhaps memory is touched upon in revision strategies given to students preparing for exams, but in our experience it is desperately lacking at the start of any learning journey, or at the heart of learning itself.

There is no doubt that teaching and learning in schools has changed dramatically over the last few decades. The traditional view of intelligence being judged on how much information can be stored and recalled at will is changing and much more value is being put on how learners can consider, explore and apply knowledge. Advances in technology have meant that we can rely on portable machines such as mobile phones, laptops, barcode scanners, and so on to do much of the storage of information for us.

## Memory and the twenty-first century learner

It is always impressive to watch people who can recite enormous amounts of information by heart, or the entire London Tube map, or Pi to 1000 places, but it is equally impressive to see people lift enormous weights. Neither are skills we particularly need in everyday life!

What we need to meet the needs of the twenty-first century are learners who are able to understand and manage their memory effectively, finding meaningful and useful ways to retain and recall learning and knowledge. Students need to feel ownership of their understanding and learning. They need to create an intimate knowledge of it so that, when recalled, it connects with other pieces of relevant knowledge in order to make comparisons and to come to conclusions.

## ASK and memory

ASK illustrates ways for students to develop an effective and efficient memory. In addition to this, it tries to outline ways in which memory might help learners organise their learning and make sense of it. We recognise that memory is complex, often subjective and linked to our emotions, but it is also the key to unlocking an individual's potential. In this chapter, we have mapped out how teachers might explicitly develop memory in useful ways so that learners can use it to manage their learning and their school lives more efficiently.

### Attitude development

| | |
|---|---|
| Resourcefulness | ✓ ✓ ✓ |
| Resilience | ✓ ✓ ✓ ✓ |
| Responsiveness | ✓ ✓ |
| Reciprocity | ✓ |
| Reflectiveness | ✓ ✓ |

# Skills and knowledge breakdown

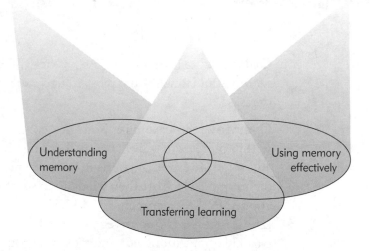

## Understanding memory

▷ Explain the difference between retention and recall
▷ Appreciate the brain's enormous capacity to remember
▷ Know the brain's different memory systems
▷ Be aware of the relative impact of the BEM principle (Beginning, End and Middle)
▷ Apply the Ebbinghaus Effect
▷ Recognise that as information is memorised it is compressed
▷ Remember that recall is an act of will
▷ Know that there is a link between recall and emotions
▷ Know about selective and distorted memories

## Using memory effectively

▷ Use multisensory strategies
▷ Plan sufficient breaks
▷ Know and use a variety of memory techniques
▷ Use a variety of ways to organise retained information and learning
▷ Go back over the material regularly

## Transferring learning

▷ Know that information has to be memorised before it can be applied
▷ Recall relevant information appropriate to the task
▷ Identify when and where to apply skills and knowledge to new situations
▷ Know when to recall relevant learning

# Learning episodes

## Learning episode 1

**Objective:** to learn how to use a variety of different strategies to support memory and to select the most effective strategy to use for different types of tasks.

**Overview:** the learning episode first considers the idea of memory within our everyday lives, before focusing on its use in school. Retention and recall are examined initially, before explanations of a number of techniques, which are then tried out in short exercises before being applied to the larger memory tasks. Students should be much more knowledgeable about strategies to use by the end of the lesson, in particular repetition, hide and seek and grouping.

### Suggested resources

**Memory techniques:**

| | |
|---|---|
| **Repetition** | Repeating the word over and over until you can recall it at will. |
| **Hide and seek** | Hiding or covering up information after trying to memorise it, then trying to recall what you want to remember without being able to see it. |
| **Grouping** | Forming groups by finding links between different parts of what is being memorised and giving each group a heading. |
| **Chunking** | Breaking down larger amounts of information to be memorised into smaller manageable 'chunks'. Similar to grouping. |
| **Association** | Remembering something unfamiliar by linking it to something you know well. |
| **Mnemonics** | Creating a memorable phrase or sentence in which each word starts with the same letter as the thing you are trying to remember; for example, to remember the order of musical notes use **E**very **G**ood **B**oy **D**eserves **F**ootball (EGBDF). |
| **Image chain/ memory walk** | Remember a list of words or objects by inventing a story in which these occur in the order you want to remember them. |

**Detailed description of learning episode 1**

Starter

1   Invite the students to think about memorable moments from their lives – for example, first days at primary and high school, birthdays – and discuss these memories with the class. Ask them some questions about where they were at exact times over the last month, using times and dates. Compare with the class how well people remember different information and whether some people remember more effectively than others.

Main learning episode

2   Before you begin, make sure you have a subject-specific learning objective requiring students to use their memory that is ready for study directly after this learning episode. In fact, you may want to introduce this to the students before teaching the episode below so that the students can make the link between what they are doing now and how they will be applying it.

3   Begin to examine what the class thinks makes some information more memorable than others and explain the importance of being able to remember things, both to successful learning at school generally and, specifically, to your subject.

4   Introduce the meaning of retention and recall and explain that they are both part of the process of remembering.

5   Show the students about 20 objects – these could be displayed on a table, or on an interactive whiteboard or just as a list. Tell the students that they have three minutes to try to remember all the objects and that you will be testing them after the three minutes. At the end of the three minutes, cover the table. Allow a few students to try recalling the items and record their efforts.

6   Encourage the students to share their experiences of trying to retain and then recall the objects and any strategies they used.

7   From the feedback and your own experience of memory, share some strategies, including one or two of the techniques of repetition, hide and seek, grouping information, mnemonics, memory walks or association (see opposite page) and introduce students to how to use them.

8   Take some time to help the students understand how the techniques work and how useful they are by letting them practise the techniques on a number of different tasks; for example, remembering the order of the planets in our solar system, remembering prime numbers or remembering the stations on a section of the London Tube.

9   Let the students have another attempt at memorising a new display of about 20 objects, stressing the importance of using one of the strategies they have been practising.

10  Discuss with the students which techniques could be useful in which settings, both in your subject and in other subjects.

### Meta-learning

1   Discuss further with the class the importance of memory in successful learning. Ask the students how they go about remembering what they learn in school and whether they try to use any particular memory strategies to help them.

## Learning episode 2

**Objective:** to develop memory further and to learn more sophisticated ways to memorise information so that it is retained effectively in long-term memory and understood.

**Overview:** the learning episode explores why repetition is such a successful technique. The episode also details a possible process for memorising in such a way that it is retained and useable when recalled. Students should be much more organised in their approach to memorising information by the end of the episode.

### Suggested resources

■   *Pelmanism or 'pairs' game* – arrange some cards with either words or pictures on them in a row, a rectangular or random formation (number of cards can be varied to differentiate the activity to suit the students' needs). Students turn over a card and then try to find its matching pair. Once a pair has been found it is removed. The student or group to match the largest number of pairs wins.

■   *Memory solitaire* – students are given a collection of objects or pictures. They are given one or two minutes to try to memorise as many as possible. The objects/pictures are then covered and students earn points by remembering as many of the objects/pictures as possible. A variation on this activity is to remove one or more items and the students must say which item(s) is missing.

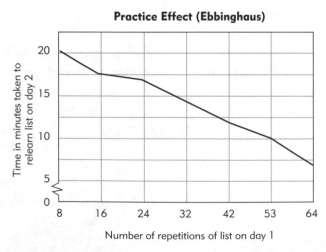

**Practice Effect (Ebbinghaus)**

*Figure 8.1 Explanation of the Ebbinghaus Effect*

### Detailed description of learning episode 2

#### Starter

1   Play 'Pairs' (see above), either as a whole class or in groups.

#### Main learning episode

2   Show students some information about a subject or subjects that they will have to memorise in order to use in their exam.

3   Give them a few minutes to memorise as much of the information as possible, reminding them of learning episode 1 and checking their recall of the techniques previously covered.

4   Question the students about which techniques they have just used, if any, and why they chose them.

5   Ask the students to predict how their recall will be affected by being shown the information repeatedly for similar lengths of time.

6   Show the students the information, test their recall again and record recall results in a table.

7   Repeat the previous step five times and plot the results on a graph to show the Ebbinghaus Effect to the class (see Figure 8.1). Discuss what the implications of this are in their learning at school in different subjects.

8   Explore the reasons why repetition is successful as a memory technique.

9   Demonstrate the science behind the theory discussed by creating a physical model of neural networking. A good method of physically presenting this is to pour a beaker of water slowly onto one end of a tray of sand, observing the pathway taken by the water and the deepening of the grooves and the distribution of the water within the sand, and relating them to how repetition helps to forge new neural connections and memories.

10  Use the strategy of grouping, that is, finding ways to group parts of the information they are trying to memorise by finding common links to help them recall the information more effectively.

11  Ask the students to give 'headings' to the groups they have created and then to make notes under the group headings. Explain that this is an example of 'chunking' the information into manageable bits and that the notes are an important part of supporting their memory.

12  Finally, give the students a chance to review their 'chunked' notes and then test them again.

### Meta-learning

1 Discuss and explore with the class the challenges faced by school students trying to organise and effectively use their memory. Focus particularly on the challenges of having so many different subjects and the time between lessons; for example, having English at the beginning of a Tuesday and not again until Friday.

2 Ask the students what the implications of the school timetable are for effective transfer of memory and application of knowledge.

## Transferring the skill and knowledge

- In all subjects it is essential to remind students of this skill and knowledge area when a new topic is introduced.
- In languages: stress the importance of and develop the use of repetition when learning new vocabulary.
- In maths: build mnemonics into retaining and recalling formulae.
- In English: memory strategies are useful to students to help memory of the different poetic techniques used by poets.

# Progression statement

When planning learning-to-learn, you will want to build progression into your schemes of learning and learning plans. In this section, we have described progression as we see it and hope this will help you map out learning-to-learn as a continuous part of your curriculum.

*As students develop into established learners, their increased understanding and awareness will be reflected as follows.*

| Transferring learning | I test my retention and recall on relevant topics regularly. I can apply information I have remembered to new tasks. I understand the part reflection plays in using what I can remember to learn new things and make progress. |
|---|---|
| Using memory effectively | I remember that recall is an act of will. I use other ways of recording information to assist my memory. I have tried different ways to remember information and made some decisions as to which are best for me. I have learned a variety of memory techniques and games. I develop notes that make it easier to remember. I know how to use my physical senses to help me remember things. I can use a wide range of long-term and short-term memory techniques for learning, including association, mnemonics, memory walks, peg words. I make demands on my memory on a regular basis. I have tested my memory and discovered that it has limits. I know that my memory strategies should suit my learning styles. I know what my concentration span is and work within it. I am careful to try to read my memory objectively, especially when remembering personal or emotional things. |
| Understanding memory | I am beginning to understand the brain's enormous capacity to remember. I can explain the difference between retention and recall. I understand that memory can be subjective. |

| | |
|---|---|
| | I have a good understanding of the science of memory. I can explain the brain's different memory systems. I can apply the Ebbinghaus Effect. I understand concentration span and the BEM principle. |

*Initially, students may connect to the learning in the following ways.*

| Transferring learning | I can recall relevant information. I know that I have to think about the things I have remembered in order to use them to learn new things and make progress. |
|---|---|
| Using memory effectively | I use repetition to help me remember new concepts and ideas. I know how to 'chunk' information to help me recall it from my memory. | I go back over material I have recently memorised. I have extended my memory of core subject knowledge. I can use the 'hide and seek' method. |
| Understanding memory | I know that it is important to remember things in order to make progress with my learning. I am aware that there are many different ways to use my memory. I understand the important part played by willpower in using my memory. I know that I have different abilities to remember different types of information depending on my interest in the subject and the type of information it is. I know that my brain has a great capacity for memory if I use the right strategy. |

# What the teachers say

'Memory is one of the most important skills when learning a new language because there is a lot of vocabulary learning taking place. Because grammatical structures are, more often than not, different in French than English, it is better to memorise longer expressions rather than single words and this requires specific memory techniques. Also, students are required to learn single words by way of vocabulary because that is what they will need to rely on for their listening and reading skills.

So far we have created several lessons in languages that aim to develop students' memory techniques. We teach the students explicitly different techniques for memorising. We use visual aids, repetition, association and "memory walk" [see page 86]. Obviously, at the end of the lesson I ask the students to reflect on which memory techniques they have learned and which were useful. We brainstorm different techniques and I ask the students to consider which techniques would be most useful to put into practice in order to prepare for a vocabulary test next week, for example. Also, I want them to generate their own skills and techniques and explain them to the rest of the class.'

*Caroline Cuinet*, French teacher

# Taking it further

It may be helpful to run some memory challenges from time to time, where students are asked not only to try to use their memory, but also to keep notes about which techniques they have used and their reasons for selecting them.

We would recommend regularly discussing with your class the importance of memory in successful learning, from remembering your timetable and what homework needs to be handed in when, to recalling relevant information when answering exam questions.

Use the different memory techniques you have introduced to your classes on a regular basis and ask the students to keep a record of how useful the technique is over a period of time in helping them remember information.

As part of your plenaries, take regular feedback from groups about how useful their technique was and how successful they were in applying it. As an alternative, you may want to give the students memory tasks and let them select which strategy they think is most useful.

Try to give students time to digest information and organise their understanding of it. In addition, encourage students to support their memory with appropriate notes.

It is helpful to test students' memory of small chunks of information on a regular basis. To help students focus as much on the development of their ability to memorise as well as their progress in the subject, it can help to sometimes show students the questions of the tests before they have to prepare for them. This way they are not overly worried about what the test will 'be like' and what will 'be in it' and can concentrate on how to remember the information.

Students seem to find using revision cards with the 'hide and seek' method particularly helpful when preparing for topics within exams.

# 9 Thinking

*'A truly great intellect is one which takes a connected view of old and new, past and present, far and near, and which has an insight into the influence of all these, one on another. It possesses the knowledge, not only of things, but also of their mutual and true relations.'*

FRED SCOTT AND JOSEPH DENNEY

## Introduction

Succeeding in helping students to think for themselves is probably the Holy Grail for every teacher and it presents a significant challenge for all of us. When we were defining the ASK curriculum it is the area that we struggled with the most; we were very interested in it but found that was hard to 'think about'. In one way a lot is known about thinking and in another way not very much. There are many fields of psychology and numerous self-help books on almost everything; all of which describe thinking processes that appear to work, but at the same time we are left with the impression that the 'science' behind them is hypothetical. Perhaps this is because thinking is that complex set of processes that take place inside the 'black box' of the brain about which we still know very little. And, furthermore, certain aspects of thinking, such as creativity, remain elusive. A century ago Ambrose Bierce cynically defined the word 'brain' as, 'an apparatus with which we think we think'. But it is the case that our understanding of our own thinking processes is limited by those very thinking processes.

A difficulty we faced when we were trying to 'hold thinking up to the light' was that all our ASK elements describe aspects of thinking. So what exactly were we talking about? At its most basic level, we thought about thinking as being the connections between nerve cells in the brain creating patterns of flow across synapses. So the elements of the ASK curriculum that are categorised under 'thinking' are related to this conceptual model of making and understanding connections. Another reason for defining it like this is that it reflects the way the academic curriculum is organised. Ultimately, when we are teaching a subject, we want our students to have an overarching concept of that subject, to see it and understand it as a piece – to understand its processes, its knowledge base, its conceptual framework. This entails creating very strong connections between aspects of the subject to develop a whole. Beyond that, within the academic curriculum, we desire that our students should see commonalities across different subjects and apply ideas and skills from one subject to another. Making links is fundamental to all of this.

Some of the most highly rated qualities in life are insight, invention, creativity, seeing new connections for the first time and creating new ideas, whether they are in science, art, economics or business. In our society, art is treasured, probably because a brilliant artist is able to show us, through drama, comedy, painting or poetry something we know but cannot quite see or express. The artist makes the connections for us.

Given all of this, it seems important that we should devise ways to help our students:

- make connections between new ideas and existing ideas.
- make connections between what might happen based on what is known.
- pick out the main ideas within a theme.
- create pictures and patterns linking new ideas together and to existing pictures and patterns within their own world.
- take existing ideas to create new ideas, by linking ideas together in different ways.

Most teachers try to employ all of these points. When we are successful as teachers with any of them, we feel great. We also know that it is disappointing when it does not work well. What are your experiences of teaching students to think? Our premise is that by introducing models of thinking in an explicit way, students are helped to learn thinking. If the processes they are going through are examined so that they can consider them, and be aware of them, students can start to be more in control of what they do. Part of the difficulty of teaching thinking is that it can be quite a painful process. To quote Bertrand Russell: 'Many people would rather die than think. In fact they do.'

As with the other skills in ASK, there is an emotional component to the cognitive process. This may be related to being on the edge of understanding and to the feelings of discomfort that arise from that. If students were aware of this, would it be more comfortable? Could students learn to enjoy those feelings? Perhaps the attitude that is most important here is Responsiveness. Recently, a colleague described her son's brilliant and interesting career that started in the arts and then moved into high-level science. She described how he was only happy when he was on the edge of what he knew. Sports psychologists also talk about the nervousness experienced before performance and their role in encouraging performers to enjoy the natural and useful feelings of nervousness. Can we teach our students to enjoy their feelings of uncertainty as they explore new connections between ideas?

## Attitude development

| Resourcefulness | ✓ ✓ ✓ ✓ |
| Resilience | ✓ ✓ ✓ |
| Responsiveness | ✓ ✓ ✓ ✓ ✓ |
| Reciprocity | ✓ |
| Reflectiveness | ✓ ✓ ✓ ✓ |

# Skills and knowledge breakdown

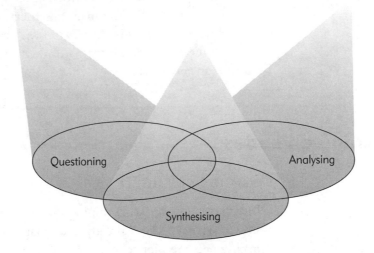

## Questioning

▷ Use questions to:
  - make predictions
  - go deeper into the subject of study
  - make connections between subjects
  - clarify understanding
  - develop a mental model of subject
▷ Organise questions into groups and sequences
▷ Select and refine questions for a particular purpose
▷ Evaluate questions after they have been used

## Analysing

▷ Use problem-solving skills
▷ Use conceptual models to explain observations
▷ Use reasoning skills
▷ Use evaluation skills

## Synthesising

▷ Within and between resources:
  - notice links between ideas and pieces of information
  - map the connections between ideas and pieces of information
  - look for contrasting and complementary ideas
▷ Classifying and mapping connections:
  - prioritise and sequence ideas and pieces of information
  - group ideas and information according to similarities and differences
  - use a variety of tools to represent the connections between ideas, such as mind maps

▷ Making connections:
  – connect new ideas and information with prior knowledge
  – create models to link ideas together
  – connect ideas and information with research question or brief
  – connect ideas and information with assessment criteria
▷ Develop new ideas

## Learning episodes

### Learning episode 1

**Objectives:** to know that thinking involves making connections between what we know already and what is new, and to know that thinking needs resilience.

**Overview:** this learning episode aims to get across the notion that thinking involves making connections. Two main tasks are involved in which the students use what they know already to solve a puzzle and to make a prediction. They have to connect the 'known' to the 'unknown'. At the end of the learning episode, the students have a 'crib sheet' of general guidance to help make connections in a range of contexts. The examples given can be replaced by those of your choice.

#### Suggested resources

- A slide of a brain
- Mystery sentence and clues for each group
- A range of examples for the students to use to make predictions.

#### Detailed description of learning episode 1

**Starter**

1  Spend five minutes playing a word association game.

2  Show a picture of the brain in order to convey the idea of making connections between nerve cells and discuss the association game.

**Main learning episode**

3  Introduce the objective for the lesson.

4  Divide the class into groups of three or four students. Give each group a set of numbered clues and a sentence with numbers in place of certain words. Ask the students to solve the sentence. The numbers on the clues are linked to the numbers in the sentence and the clues allow students to 'solve the sentence'.

For example, use clues to solve the sentence:

**'1 is an 2 3 4. In 5 we use 6 to 7 us to make 1.'**

Clues are pictures. '1' is weather forecasting; '2' is the headteacher; '3' is the brain; '4' is a picture of footballer (Michael Owen kicking a ball); '5' is Einstein; '6' is a picture of Kate Moss; '7' is the SOS sign. Extra clues can be available if students get stuck, but there should be penalties for using these. The same idea can be used with different sorts of clue. (Adapted from Ginnis 2002.)

## Meta-learning

1  Discuss with the class the process of 'making connections' that is involved in 'solving the sentence'. Compare it to the word association game at the start of the learning episode.

2  Draw out the importance of needing resilience to persevere to find the answer.

3  Take the sentence that was derived using the clues and use it to explore thinking further. The sentence can be one of your own choosing. In the example above, the sentence should read: *'Predicting is an important thinking skill. In science we use models to help us make predictions.'*

4  Give the students a range of examples of incomplete information and ask them to make predictions. Useful examples are: a number of mathematical shapes that are unfinished; a short paragraph of text where letters in the middle of words have been missed out or turned into symbols; a familiar piece of music that stops before a phrase has finished; obscure words and definitions that need to be matched; figures that need to be matched with items, such as the length of time it takes for different materials to biodegrade; a film extract where students decide what happens next.

5  At the end of the exercise, the result should be similar but with different predictions made by different groups.

6  Discuss the predictions with the class and how they make predictions.

7  Finish the learning episode by devising some questions, with the students, to use to help make predictions. For example:
   - What do I know about this already?
   - What ideas are linked to this?
   - How many different predictions can I make?

## Learning episode 2

**Objectives:** to develop the skill of questioning to be able to choose effective questions to make predictions, and to know that resourcefulness is important in thinking.

**Overview:** the second learning episode aims to develop students' questioning skills in order to help them connect what they already know to what they need to find out. The example provided is of a history lesson, but the same method could be used in other subjects. A simple method is used, based on the game 'twenty questions' in which students work out the name of a historical figure. Students are encouraged to think about the questions they ask and which ones are most effective.

### Suggested resources

- Pens
- A1 paper
- Blu-tack
- Pictures of relevant historical figures
- Sticky notes
- Flipchart

### Detailed description of learning episode 2

#### Starter

1   Show the students artefacts and a number of pictures from a specific period in history and ask them to think of as many links as they can between the artefacts and pictures.

2   Take ideas from the students and use this as a lead into recalling what they have learned about connecting ideas and into the main lesson objective to come next.

#### Main learning episode

3   Take a theme that the students are studying and ask the students to brainstorm, individually and then as a class, all the important historical figures associated with the theme. Recap important facts about these people and display the facts in the room. Examples for different subjects could include: an art lesson – famous artists; a science lesson – elements in the periodic table; a maths lesson – geometrical figures; a French lesson – vocabulary of a topic.

4   Arrange the students in pairs. Give one student a picture of a historical figure. The other student then asks their partner ten questions to which the answer can only be 'yes' or 'no'. Get the students to compete to see who can find the answer using the fewest questions.

### Meta-learning

1   Ask the students to work in their pairs to think about the questions they asked. Which ones worked well? Which ones less well? Ask them to put the questions on sticky notes of two different colours: good questions go on one colour, less good on another colour. Create a large table with two columns on the board or a flip chart and ask the student to put their sticky notes of good questions in one column and less good questions in the other column.

2   Discuss the questions that worked well and why. Bring out the importance of resourcefulness.

3   Try doing the same task again using different pictures or other material. Ask the students to use what they learned in order to think carefully about their questions.

4   Finish by discussing the differences this time and note any important points to remember.

## Transferring the skill and knowledge

Summarise the thinking processes the students have learned in previous lesson episodes and create a crib card to help the transfer of skills to other lessons.

# Progression statement

When planning learning-to-learn, you will want to build progression into your schemes of learning and learning plans. In this section, we have described progression as we see it and hope this will help you map out learning-to-learn as a continuous part of your curriculum.

**Synthesising**
- I can map the connections between ideas to develop mental models of a group of ideas.
- I can link ideas across different subjects and broad areas within a subject.
- I can connect ideas to assessment criteria.
- I can connect ideas to a research brief.
- I can link ideas together to create a complete evaluation of tasks, procedures, investigations, products, problems and so on.
- I can develop new ideas.

**Analysing**
- I can use problem-solving skills to help me approach tasks.
- I can use conceptual models to explain observations.
- I can use evaluation skills to make judgements.

**Questioning**
- I can devise and use questions to go deeper into a subject and to link ideas between subjects.
- I can use questions to help me develop mental models of ideas.
- I can use questions to evaluate information.

*As students develop into established learners, their increased understanding and awareness will be reflected as follows.*

**Synthesising**
- I can map the connections between ideas and pieces of information.
- I can group information and identify contrasting and complementary ideas.
- I can sequence ideas.
- I can represent the links between ideas by using mind maps and similar tools.

**Analysing**
- I can use reasoning skills to make inferences from information.
- I can notice links between ideas and pieces of information.

**Questioning**
- I can devise questions and use them to help me make predictions, to clarify my understanding and to make connections between my existing knowledge and new material.

*Initially, students may connect to the learning in the following ways.*

# What the teachers say

'Thinking comes into all PE lessons. The students have to work out what skill to use, how they should use it and why. For example, if the students are playing basketball and one student tries to pass to another but the ball ends up going to a member of the opposition, we ask the students to think about why that happened and what they can do to avoid it next time.

We do a lot of questioning, not just at the end of the lesson, but all the way through the lesson. We ask questions such as, "The opposition are quite a strong team, how do you think you are going to beat them?" or "That student looked like they would win the long distance race. What happened? What can you learn from this?" The questions are not just about skills they are about tactics as well.

We encourage the students to think ahead – something they find very difficult particularly in Year 7. One of the first things we do with Year 7 is to get them to dribble a ball and then stop. We point out that some people keep the ball close to them when they dribble and others don't. We ask, "What are the advantages of the keeping the ball close," and then we encourage students to think about how they can do that. We like to let them have a go, make mistakes and then analyse by talking and thinking and demonstrating. More recently, I have been giving the students "thinking time" – I ask them to think about points and then I ask questions a few minutes later. The very first learning-to-learn lesson we do is on thinking and it involves a batting team and a fielding team. The students have to develop the best strategy they can and they try things out and we talk about them and then they try again. It works very well.'

*Martin Baillie*, Head of PE

'Thinking in drama is important when evaluating drama. We introduce evaluation with Year 7 students and they find it difficult to articulate their thoughts. Even though they can follow a piece of drama and enjoy it, they find it almost impossible to talk about it. It seems difficult even to say things like, "This was good because it was funny." During the year, we build up the students' vocabulary and they get better at evaluation as they are more able to describe what they mean.

With older students, evaluation is also a challenging area. They have to go to a deeper level and understand the use of symbolism. We help them to develop this by introducing props and symbols that they have to use to devise a short drama. They watch each other's piece and then analyse it and evaluate it. In this way, we move from their own experience to a practical experience to an objective evaluation.

Another area of drama that brings in thinking is in creating characters and we use a range of techniques here; for example, giving the students three objects that were found in the hand luggage of someone who died in a plane crash. The students have to create a character consistent with the objects. We "hot seat" the students and they have to make sure their character is consistent. Another technique we use to develop "thinking in character" is to set up scenarios and each character has an objective that determines their behaviour. For example, a group of characters are stranded on a desert island: one character is frightened but loves the colour green; another character wants to get as far away as possible from the first character; a third character is in love with the second character and so on. This works very well.'

*Helen McGrath*, drama teacher

## Taking it further

Show how theoretical models can be used to make predictions. For example, particle models; maths models; models of how to create stories (English); models of historical events; models of grammar learned to predict newly introduced grammar; models of musical form to compose new music; models of body shape and design to predict the best clothes for an individual.

In PE, study the tactics used by the students' favourite sports teams. Before a match predict what will happen. Invite the students to analyse the opposing team and suggest the tactics their team should play. Set a 'panel' of experts to comment on a game before or after it is played. For school games use the reserve team to watch inter-school matches. Ask them to analyse the game and give feedback.

In drama, explore 'The Set' for a devised piece that will be consistent with each of the characters and that will help the students to see their peers as characters. Spend time developing ideas that are in harmony with each of the characters and how they can be represented in direct and symbolic ways. Use this to reflect on techniques for staying in character during a performance.

# 10 Adapting

*'How did I do, miss?'*
*'You got a level 4.'*
*'But that's what I got last test. What's the point? I always get the same level!'*

Albert Einstein is credited with saying that his definition of madness was doing the same thing in the same way again and again yet expecting a different outcome, but being disappointed when nothing changed. And yet if this really is madness, then most of us are truly insane.

If we are honest, we do not reflect on most of the things we do or the way we do them, nor do we evaluate our performance and make the necessary changes to do it better next time. Partly because we are too busy getting on with doing things and partly because although we know we could do better, we are not entirely sure how to go about making the necessary changes. We do something the way we do it for a reason. And that reason is normally so much a part of our fabric, part of our routine, that it is just the way we do it. We cannot analyse it or separate it from ourselves sufficiently to change. The way we do things seems a bit like a part of our behaviour. It is our strategy for coping with the demands of our life and it is only when it breaks down and real problems arise that we do something about trying to change. And how do most of us go about adapting and making changes? We consult a third party such as a friend, a coach or a counsellor.

It makes sense that students will find it tremendously difficult to change and adapt their learning. They approach tasks a certain way and learn a certain way based on years of having certain factors reinforced and made routine. They too develop their coping strategies and it can be extremely difficult to encourage students to have the confidence to adapt. Added to this is often the issue of a student's self-esteem and how they feel about themselves with that particular learning matter. This can explain why certain students find it hard to make the necessary changes in subjects they struggle in. It is easier to convince themselves that they do not like the subject, or the teacher, rather than face the issue that they themselves have a problem, or are the problem. Another effect of low self-esteem can result in students burying their heads in the sand and ignoring bad results and critical feedback, choosing to carry on blindly without any review of evaluating, therefore avoiding the risk of further damaging their opinion of themselves.

Making progress, improving, succeeding, getting it right, becoming an expert, doing it well, passing, the list could go on, but it is knowing what, when and how to make appropriate or suitable changes to the way we do things that is the key. It is a real challenge and one that is often underestimated. When asked about this skill, a Year 8 student spontaneously replied:

> 'Adapting and making progress often takes a long time. You're used to how you learn and it takes time to change. Imagine moving house from somewhere you've lived for a long time. You're used to the old place and where things are and suddenly you're somewhere new. It can be scary and you'll often feel like going back to the way you used to do things before.'

We believe the students need to have a certain level of expertise to know what to change, when to change it and how to go about changing. The challenge is to develop this level of analytical expertise in students about themselves and their learning.

## Attitude development

| | |
|---|---|
| Resourcefulness | ✓ ✓ |
| Resilience | ✓ ✓ ✓ ✓ |
| Responsiveness | ✓ ✓ ✓ ✓ ✓ |
| Reciprocity | ✓ |
| Reflectiveness | ✓ ✓ ✓ ✓ |

# Skills and knowledge breakdown

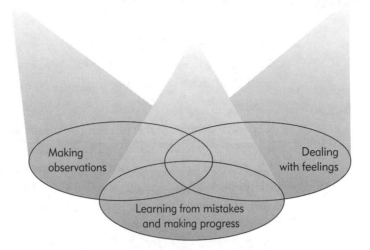

## Making observations

▷ Watch and learn from others around you
▷ Try to select and apply positive strategies for learning
▷ Identify what needs to change

## Dealing with feelings

▷ Accept valid positive feedback without dismissing or diluting the message
▷ Let success feed your feelings of personal pride (self-esteem) and your motivation to achieve even greater things
▷ Accept valid negative feedback without defending or excusing yourself
▷ Write action steps to achieve targets
▷ Select development areas from self-evaluation and feedback from others
▷ Turn development areas into SMART targets
▷ Monitor your personal action plan and re-plan where necessary

## Learning from mistakes and making progress

▷ Analyse mistakes and amend future behaviour/actions accordingly
▷ Evaluate the usefulness of feedback
▷ Avoid blaming circumstances or other people for issues that are under your own control
▷ Know how and when to apply new strategies

# Learning episodes

## Learning episode 1

**Objective:** to gain knowledge and expertise about different ways to try so that students are making the best decisions to ensure that progress is made.

**Overview:** during this learning episode the students have the opportunity to change their minds, make wrong decisions and try to make use of what they learn from the experience. The episode blends fun elements from television games shows and quiz shows to look at models and useful processes for being successful.

### Suggested resources

The activity used for the main learning episode is a version of the 1970s children's game show *Runaround*.

1   Organise the room so that there is an open area for students to move around in. Take three pieces of A2 or A3 paper and write the letter 'A' on one, 'B' on the second and 'C' on the third. Place them either on a wall or the floor separate from each other.

2   Explain to the class that they are going to play a version of an old TV quiz called *Runaround*. You will ask them a question and each student will have 30 seconds to decide which of the three answers given is correct – A, B or C. After the 30 seconds they should go and stand by the piece of paper displaying the appropriate letter. After they have decided, they are given another 30 seconds to decide if they want to stick with their choice or change and stand by another answer. The students who are standing by the wrong letters after they have had the chance to change their minds must now sit down and the next question applies only to those left standing. The round is over when you have one person remaining who is the winner.

3   Ask quite complicated 'general knowledge' questions, each with three answers.

4   After five or six rounds, ask the group to take their seats and discuss the game with them, exploring what was helpful about having the chance to see and consider other students' answers and to be able to change their mind. You may want to discuss any tactics used by the students who did well and lasted quite a few questions into each round as well as looking at the pros and cons of going with the majority vote each time.

An alternative way to play the game is to use mini whiteboards or sheets with A, B and C written on them and the students hold them up. The only problem with this is losing the sense of being able to see people actually changing their mind.

### Detailed description of learning episode 1

#### Starter

1   Use the starter to discuss being a success. It may be helpful to explore the strategies and methods successful people use. Focusing particularly on taking risks, making mistakes, making changes, using the opinions and ideas of others, relying upon themselves can be helpful. The following can be useful examples:
    a)   Television quiz shows, such as *Who Wants To Be A Millionaire*, *Deal or No Deal* and *Play Your Cards Right*.
    b)   Successful business leaders such as Richard Branson, Anita Roddick and Alan Sugar.
    c)   Television shows such as *Dragon's Den* and *The Apprentice*.

2   Try to link the discussion with the strategies, methods and risks a good learner might need to take in order to be successful.

#### Main learning episode

3   Play a version of the 1970s children's game show *Runaround* with the class. For detailed rules about the activity, read the explanation in the resources section above. This activity can be run as a physical exercise with students moving around the room to demonstrate their choices or with students sat at desks displaying their choices on mini whiteboards or pieces of paper.

    Note: It is equally possible to achieve the learning objective for this part of the episode by running your own game show or a version of one of the television game shows listed in the starter.

4   During this activity, try to ask varied and challenging questions; each time, remember to give one correct answer and two incorrect answers. Use general knowledge questions for this stage of the learning episode.

5   After five or six rounds, ask the class to take their seats and discuss the game with them. Find out what was helpful about having the chance to discuss their ideas and change their minds. Encourage the students to really think about their feelings during the game and find out how they felt when they were right, when they were wrong and when they were deciding whether to change their minds.

6   The next section of the learning episode builds on the previous activity and should use a topic from your own subject. Put students into groups of three and explain the aims and rules of the activity. Students should try to collect as many points as possible by answering the questions about the specific topic. When they are asked a question,

they have a choice either to answer the question themselves with no conferring and if they are right, they earn five points; or they can choose to confer with the others in their group and if they are right, they earn only three points. An extra level of complexity can be added by keeping one member of the group completely separate with some information to refer to. The student being asked the question can consult this member, but will only get one point if they are right.

7    It can be useful to represent how each group is doing physically by using a whiteboard or by using the students themselves!

### Meta-learning

1    Discuss with the class the importance of thinking through decisions and ideas, adapting your thinking and answers, and making necessary changes. Explore with the class the difficulties of this and why we find adapting difficult.

2    Ask the groups to reflect upon how often in lessons they get the opportunity, or make the opportunity, to reflect on their performances in different subjects and to decide what changes to make.

## Learning episode 2

**Objective:** to understand the importance of reviewing decisions and making changes in being successful.

**Overview:** during this learning episode the students have the opportunity to learn from their mistakes and to avoid repeating them.

### Suggested resources

1    Pictures and descriptions of tropical islands.

2    Pictures of people and animals burying their heads in the sand.

**Figure 10.1 Example picture of a tropical island**

### Detailed description of learning episode 2

**Starter**

1. Explore with the class the frustration that students often feel when they are not making any progress. Ask the question: 'Why do you think that we often repeat the same mistakes over and over again?'

2. Discuss the benefits and drawbacks of living the same day over and over again – focus on frustrations, liberations, resilience, risk taking, adapting and improving. If you know it, use the film *Groundhog Day* as a focus to begin with. Try watching parts of the film with the class in a lesson beforehand or choose to summarise the story.

### Main learning episode

3. Explain that you are going to give the class the opportunity to live a 'pretend day' over and over again. Encourage them to be adventurous, but also to reflect on their decisions.

4. Put the class into groups of four and set the scene. They are travelling on a boat near the equator that hits a reef and sinks. They swim to safety on a nearby island that is remote and looks tropical and uninhabited. On the beach they meet three other survivors.

5. This is optional, but the description in the first chapter of *Lord of the Flies* by William Golding is a good basis for what the island might look like. However, you may want to use pictures of tropical islands to help the students to visualise where they are imagining they are (see Figure 10.1).

6. Give the groups a list of professions, such as builder, farmer, fitness instructor, chef, scientist, doctor, teacher, and ask them to choose a role each. You may want to brainstorm further lists of what skills the group has. For example, a chef would be skilled at cutting, planning, organising, leading people and would have some science knowledge, such as food nutrition and health.

7. Ask the groups to make three decisions about what they are going to do to survive their first day on the island. They must bring their decisions to you for assessment.

8. Assess each group's decisions with them – try to give one positive and one negative assessment and feedback for each decision. Ask the groups to evaluate their decisions and conclude upon the success of their first day. Remind the group of *Groundhog Day* and ask them to run the whole day differently, including choosing group members, basing their decisions on what did and did not go well on the day before. Remind the groups of the importance of adapting and improving.

**9** Again, assess each group's decisions and ask groups to evaluate at the end.

**10** Ask the groups to compare the successes and failures of the two first days and to explain the differences and reasons for them. Explore the idea of running the same day for a third time.

### Meta-learning

**1** Show students pictures of people and animals burying their heads in the sand, and discuss what we mean by this expression.

**2** Discuss with the class why students might ignore bad news and failure at school.

## Transferring the skill and knowledge

In all subjects, it is essential to build in strategies to link this skill and knowledge area to when assessment is given, both formative and summative, formal and informal.

# Progression statement

When planning learning-to-learn, you will want to build progression into your schemes of learning and learning plans. In this section, we have described progression as we see it and hope this will help you map out learning-to-learn as a continuous part of your curriculum.

| | |
|---|---|
| **Learning from mistakes and making progress** | I understand that sometimes things that are important may take a while to achieve.<br>I remind myself that failure can be a step to future success and will have another go before giving up.<br>I understand that I can learn from the success of others and sometimes ask friends for guidance.<br>I am beginning to realise when I can help others with things they find difficult and sometimes offer help.<br>I use the feedback I receive, even when it is critical, to plan my ideas and work generally.<br>I actively seek to hear people's ideas and am happy to discuss their criticisms of my work.<br>I use my mistakes and failures to help me succeed. |
| **Dealing with feelings** | I do not let failure in one area affect my overall performance, effort or self-esteem.<br>I am honest about and take responsibility for my failures and mistakes. I do not look to blame others.<br>I am not afraid of looking at myself as part of the problem and making changes to my attitude.<br>I do not see making early mistakes or initial failure in any project or work as an overall failure.<br>I always try to reflect on the reasons why I have failed and then plan to try again.<br>I do not shy away from discussing people's failures and disappointments.<br>I am careful how I phrase things when I am talking to people about their disappointments.<br>I am not personal in my criticism, making sure that I discuss the work not the person.<br>I understand that failure can make people sensitive and upset. |
| **Making observations** | I know success mostly comes from hard work.<br>I often reflect on successful pieces of work to inform me about how I might go about new pieces of work or projects.<br>I try to celebrate in an appropriate manner and at an appropriate time.<br>I know that I can learn from failure by setting myself targets to improve. |

*As students develop into established learners, their increased understanding and awareness will be reflected as follows.*

| | |
|---|---|
| **Learning from mistakes and making progress** | I use the teacher as a resource for feedback.<br>I know that I must listen to feedback, both positive and critical, to help me improve.<br>I try not to ignore feedback if it is critical of me or my work.<br>I try not to get upset or annoyed when people criticise my work. |
| **Dealing with feelings** | I understand that it is important to be resilient.<br>I know that I should want others to succeed.<br>I try to listen to the feedback about work I have done badly in even if I want to forget about it and move on.<br>I try not to use the failure of others to take the pressure off myself.<br>I often help friends if they are struggling.<br>I do not join in making fun of people who are finding things difficult. |
| **Making observations** | I want to be successful in my school life.<br>I am aware that critical feedback and assessment can produce a variety of different reactions in people.<br>I am aware that when I am successful, it is natural to want to celebrate.<br>I try not to get upset when I don't do well.<br>I understand that I may need to change some of my habits and routines. |

*Initially, students may connect to the learning in the following ways.*

## What the teachers say

'For anything to work, I think it has to be taught again and again and the learner has to know why they're doing it. Even with stuff like Brain Gym® I find that students have been doing it at primary school, but they're not really sure why they're doing it. It is not until students have a clear idea of what they're doing and the reasons behind it that they'll really begin to take any sort of charge of it themselves. We found the same thing with asking questions. The first hurdle to get over was to explain the importance of questioning in the learning process, and the next was to teach the kids how to ask effective questions. Once that's in place changes can begin to be made. The kids appreciate it when I acknowledge that I've made mistakes or I'm learning from them. If I present myself as the fountain of all wisdom and it is like a closed, finite thing, then that's just going to give them the opinion that learning's like that. We should be trying to instil in them life learning and lifelong learning. I say all the time to them, the reason I teach is because I love learning and I'm learning all the time.'

*Paul Craven*, Head of Geography

## Taking it further

Use any opportunities that involve giving feedback to students or assessing students' work formatively to make sure they understand the key assessment criteria before they begin to plan how to improve.

Use well-known historical figures as examples of those who have responded and adapted effectively and those who have not. Explore their successes and failures and draw out any key learning points.

Using Darwin's theory of evolution and the survival of the fittest to explore the importance of adapting successfully to changes. Equally effective can be taking examples of technological development as a stimulus for discussion and learning about adapting; for example, the progression from gramophone to ipod.

Explore the relationship between adapting and the attitude of responsiveness. Using the well-known saying, 'If at first you don't succeed, try, try again', look at the importance of resilience and responsiveness in making progress, successfully breaking routines and dealing with change. You may also want to encourage students to write their own, twenty-first-century sayings to promote the attributes you have been discussing.

It is important to give students opportunities to discover the strategies they use to learn and the routines and learning patterns they have established in your subject. In order to adapt and make progress, they will need to explore the origins of these strategies, routines and patterns and decide whether they are successful or not and how they can be adapted. They need to be given time and opportunities to attempt the risky business of trying to develop new ways of learning and most essentially be encouraged to see failure as an important part of the learning process.

Discuss with students things they have achieved so far in their lives and share good ideas and the strategies they used. During these discussions, focus on areas of success that were near failures or that involved a lot of failure before being successful.

# 11 Co-constructing learning with students

*'The joy of learning is as indispensable in study as breathing is in running. Where it is lacking there are no real students, but only poor caricatures of apprentices who, at the end of their apprenticeship, will not even have a trade.'*

SIMONE WEIL

## COMING UP IN THIS CHAPTER

▶ An introduction to co-constructing learning with students.
▶ Practical suggestions of generic techniques to use in developing and increasing student responsibility for learning.

The ultimate aim of a learning-to-learn curriculum is to equip students with the tools to become independent and lifelong learners. Chapters 4–10 describe how to teach the separate skills of our ASK curriculum and this chapter attempts to take learning-to-learn a step further to suggest ways in which your students can become partners with you to construct their own learning experiences. Although this is the focus of the 'Taking it further' sections of Chapters 4–10, we felt that this was so crucial to the long-term success of learning-to-learn that the subject warranted a further chapter. In this chapter, we suggest practical ways in which you can shift responsibility for leading learning from you as the teacher towards the students, so they are equal and active participants in creating their own learning experiences.

Below, Juliet recounts the following reflection from observing a Year 7 lesson:

> 'When I was observing an art lesson, the teacher introduced her students to the learning outcomes at the beginning of the lesson. She asked each student to rate their performance on each of the learning outcomes on a scale from one to five. She asked them to do this 40 minutes into a three-hour lesson so that they could assess their progress before moving on. The students listened attentively to their teacher, understood what she said and when she finished they all ignored her instructions and carried on with what they were doing beforehand. As I watched this, I wondered why this happened and what she could have done to encourage the students to engage in assessing their own learning.'

In developing learning-to-learn within your own classroom, you may wish to consider the implications for your role as a teacher and to start to think about how to shift responsibility onto students. This chapter offers some ideas and techniques to help you with this. In fact, in writing this chapter we wondered whether it might provide our readers with a good starting point for developing learning-to-learn in their own classroom before embarking on teaching the Attitudes, Skills and Knowledge described in Chapters 4–10.

## Time management and learning

1   At the start of a lesson, share the time management with your students. Instead of giving them a series of short timed deadlines throughout the lesson – for example, 'You have five minutes to finish this task' – explain how a one-hour lesson will be divided up and provide the desired outcomes of each section. Use an actual clock face with moveable hands to illustrate this or a diagram of a clock face divided into sections.

Alternatively, ask each student or group of students to decide how long they think they need in order to achieve different learning outcomes and invite them to draw their own clock to show how they will manage their time in the lesson.

Create opportunities for students to take responsibility for monitoring the use of time by nominating two students to be 'time monitors' or 'time police'. They keep track of what students are doing and move them on when their time is up. Rotate the role around the class so that all students have the chance to practise this skill.

2   Give students a sense of how time will be used throughout the year to teach their course by, for example, having a large wall chart of the scheme of learning to show how it develops throughout the year, the month, the week.

3   Introduce physical resources to help students monitor time. For example, a large sandtimer, a digital timer projected onto a whiteboard or a clock face with multiple and moveable hands in the student planner.

4   Introduce opportunities for students to plan their use of time in a broader arena than in the classroom. For example, ask them to consider how they use their time during a normal week and then once they have listed all the different activities that they do, divide them into those that they:
   - 'must do' – eating, sleeping, washing
   - 'have to do' – their share of household duties, coming to school
   - 'need to do' – completing their homework
   - 'want to do' – playing with friends, staying fit, planning a holiday, getting a part-time job.

Ask them to consider how much of their own time is within their own control and whether and how they can get more control of their time.

## Booking times to see the teacher

To help students to develop their time-management strategies and to encourage them to be strategic in their use of the teacher as a resource, at Villiers, we try to make it a learning habit to ask students to book their time with the teacher in advance. This will include booking details about when in a lesson they need to see the teacher and how long they need to spend with them. As a further development of this idea, it can be effective to use the booking form yourself, so that if, for instance, you want to speak to the whole class about a particular subject, then this can be blocked out on the booking form. (For further information about using booking forms, see Ginnis 2002.)

An example of a booking sheet is provided in Figure 11.1.

**Teacher's Time Planner**

| Teacher's time | Dates of lessons | Start of lesson |
|---|---|---|
| 5 mins | | |
| 10 mins | | |
| 15 mins | | |
| 20 mins | | |
| 25 mins | | |
| 30 mins | | |
| 35 mins | | |
| 40 mins | | |
| 45 mins | | |
| 50 mins | | |
| End of lesson | | |

**Figure 11.1**

## Assessment and learning

1  Some students prefer to be assessed by tests and exams, while others prefer coursework. At the beginning of a new topic or new school year, ask each student to elect how they will be assessed on the topic.

Develop this further and ask students to elect the method of assessment they think is most appropriate for different elements of a topic. For example: written test; observation of practical task; question and answer using mini whiteboards; teacher conducting an in-depth interview with each student; a project; an extended piece of writing; a physical model or finished product; a series of diagrams or pictures; peer assessment; self-assessment.

Invite students to decide when they are ready to be assessed.

2   Create the conditions for assessment and practise the process by sharing assessment objectives and criteria for assessment. Ask students to assess and evaluate their own learning and that of others on a regular basis. Include events outside the classroom, such as football games, tennis matches, programmes on TV, films, newspaper and magazine articles, and your own lessons and lesson plans.

3   Develop 'learning triads', where three students take on the separate roles of learning coach, learning critic and learner. Encourage each student to take on each role in turn so that they all get the opportunity to assess each other and to help each other learn. It will be important to create the right atmosphere for learning in the classroom before using this technique (see page 127).

## Planning with students

1   At the beginning of the year, share the full year's scheme of learning with the class. Discuss the broad learning outcomes for the year and the order of topics. Be open to suggestions from students to change the order of topics.

Spend some time with students at the beginning of a course to allow them to construct their own plan to create the linkages between the main themes of their syllabus; for example, put the key themes in an envelope, ask students to work in groups to debate how they link them together, then when they are happy with their plan, ask them to stick it onto paper to make a poster and display this on the wall. This is their own personal plan of their learning for the year. Students can refer to it during lessons throughout the year to see where they are and where they are going next.

2   Start a topic by planning the learning with the students. Introduce key questions and ask students to plan how they want to investigate and answer these questions. Offer choice to allow different students to do things in different ways, agree on timescales and key outcomes. Agree any common learning experiences to be shared by the whole class. Ensure that key misconceptions are addressed through well-planned activities, experiences, models and questions (for more guidance on this, see 'Blank Cheque' and 'Stepometer' in Ginnis 2002).

## Setting up L-bay

Create a website where students can raise questions and have them answered by other students. Introduce a rating system so that students can rate the answers they get. Use an existing on-line community such as Think.com so that students can interact with others throughout the world.

# Creating physical resources to help

In trying to maximise the opportunities to develop the students' attitudes, skills and knowledge you may decide it is useful to create physical resources. These can often help students actually use their learning-to-learn skills as well as acting as a visual prompt or reminder. Any visual image that readily and universally symbolises something is worth spending some time developing and you may wish to involve the students in creating ideas for these resources and in actually making them.

In the list below, some resources are easily made, while others require more time and possibly outsourcing to professional companies.

First, create a *Learning Wall* that should be a permanent display and is used, added to and developed on a regular basis. This can act as a resource centre for learning-to-learn as well as a useful visual reference for all students during their learning experiences in that classroom. If this is something that is created in classrooms across the school and to a standard format, then the transferability of learning-to-learn will be reinforced. Some of the displays on a Learning Wall could include the following.

- *Clock with moving hands* – use to illustrate the importance of time management and to develop more independent timekeeping, especially if the students are given responsibility to either set time limits for different parts of a lesson or asked to monitor the time management of the lesson.
- *Noisometer* – use to represent different levels of noise from silent or independent learning time, through acceptable group-work discussion noise, to unacceptable and disturbing noise. As with the clock above, if responsibility for this is given to students, either a pair to monitor the whole class or a single member of each group during collaborative learning, then it can help develop more independence and self-discipline.
- *Big question mark* – use to symbolise 'Question Time'.
- *Light bulb* – use to symbolise 'Ideas Time'.
- *Magnifying glass* – use to symbolise 'Research Time'.
- *Brain* – use to symbolise 'Thinking Time'.
- *Group role badges* – such as spokesperson, note-taker, chief researcher, group leader, timekeeper, illustrator, organiser, ideas-maker. These are useful to have on display; the ones relevant to the learning task should be shared out by students working in groups. Another group of roles might be learner, learning critic, learning coach – these are particularly useful roles to make explicit during peer assessment. As simple as it may sound, the more explicit the role, the more likely students are to feel confident to play the role, especially if the class have done some work developing the skills and the teacher has modelled good practice.
- *Different group types* – as above, with the group role badges, displaying headings for different types of groups helps students think about the different types of groups they could work in and relate choices about who to work with to the criteria of what they are trying to achieve. Group types include ability, friendship, random and so on.

- *Room layouts for different group activities* – displaying and sharing information with students about how the physical space can be used for different types of learning experiences can be powerful and is also a really useful way of getting students involved in setting out the classroom for learning. For example, explain the learning activities planned and then ask the students to prepare the room from the layouts displayed. Designs displayed should include layouts for paired assessment work, group-work, debating forum, circle layouts for question times and discussions, presentations, carousel activities, research time.

- *Learning-to-learn attitudes, skills and knowledge* – if everyone can easily see the headings, terminology and keywords of learning-to-learn, then it is far more likely that it will get regular use.

Second, create some physical resources to help students review, reflect and evaluate their learning. It is generally accepted that assessment of and for learning is an essential part of effective teaching and learning, but how to do it regularly with the students and in meaningful ways is something that can prove extremely challenging to even the most experienced teacher. The ideas below are examples of visual and engaging ways to involve students in regularly assessing their learning outcomes, the progress they are making and their feelings towards the lesson.

- *Ladders* – using an image of a ladder can be effective because it is an easily recognisable metaphor for making progress. Having a standard image (possibly magnetic for a whiteboard) or a 3D model of a ladder to display on a whiteboard for students to use can be useful when asking students to track the progress they are making with their learning. Alternatively, using the frame of a ladder where students fit in rungs to show their own progression is an even more interactive way to assess learning. A further extension to this idea is to give all students mini-ladders that they can use regularly in self-assessment.

- *Steps* – another great image that instantly symbolises a progressive journey is a series of steps or a staircase. Progressive learning outcomes could be written alongside rising steps and students could be encouraged to spend time reviewing their journey. This resource is easily combined with the ladders above as a way of recognising that students will find some 'learning steps' difficult to climb in one go and may need some additional smaller steps. The image of the ladder propped up against a step can be used to help students illustrate where they have needed help or support. Additionally, both can be used at the start of a learning journey. It is helpful for the students to think about and plan the learning objectives a teacher has set, the difficulties they think might arise and the support and help they think they might need.

- *Thermometers* – this resource is designed to explore with the students their engagement in and enjoyment of the lesson. This can easily be used in comparison with either the ladder or steps above to explore the relationship between engagement and progress. Just as with a real thermometer, the idea here is for the students to take the temperature of the lesson, which can also lead to very open discussions with students about reasons why they were or were not engaged in their learning. This is a type of reflection that, if done regularly, can lead to the co-construction of future learning experiences.

Third, as an attempt to wet the appetite and get the creative juices of any learning-to-learn enthusiast flowing, we offer the following as starters.

- *Learning-to-learn Rubik cubes* – using the seven skills and five attitudes. We all know how our hands and minds often work in subliminary unity, so why not keep the frantic hands and minds of students busy with a puzzle that should cement the ideas and vocabulary of learning-to-learn.
- *Snakes and ladders* – even in this technological age, board games are still enormously popular. Specially adapting this classic is a great way to encourage students to be enthusiastic about a particular learning journey and to be realistic and honest in identifying potential hindrances (snakes) as well as achievement and progression (ladders). This works particularly well in trying to develop students' awareness of the importance of the attitudes.
- *Jigsaw puzzles* – this is another timelessly classic puzzle that can be designed to challenge students to think about how learning-to-learn attitudes, skills and knowledge can be mapped out for different learning experiences and to see the connections between them together.
- *Learning 'Lego' blocks* – by creating learning-to-learn bricks, perhaps with attitudes, skills and knowledge in different colours or with words printed on the side of the bricks, this becomes an interactive and very 3D way of seeing how to build good learning and also seeing links and making connections between different areas of learning-to-learn.

Finally, we suggest creating a *learning toolbox*. The *Skills* of the ASK curriculum can be seen as analogous to tools that may be selected and used appropriately to solve a given problem or complete a task. One way that may prove to be beneficial could be to create a physical 'toolbox' in a convenient corner or space in the classroom. This means that the students can freely visit it as a resource to help them progress in their learning. This might usefully sit alongside a laptop or other networked PC with internet access as an aid to developing the students' *resourcefulness*. To take this idea further, you might wish to create an electronic version of this toolbox containing e-versions of all 'step-by-step guides', writing frames, group roles, keywords and so on. For the adventurous and committed teacher, the 'e-toolbox' might contain video-streaming demonstrations of not only subject-specific skills and techniques but also video clips demonstrating generic learning skills and elements of knowledge from the ASK curriculum

The contents of the toolbox could clearly be varied according to the needs of the particular students or the demands of a particular curriculum area but might usefully include some or all of the following:

- A step-by-step guide to 'Investigating Resources'
- A list of the different types of groups, the advantages and disadvantages of each and roles within a group
- An adaptation of Guy Claxton's 'Stuck Poster'
- A stopwatch or other timing device

- Coloured counters, dice, playing cards and so on
- Dictionary and thesaurus
- Writing frames including an action plan pro-forma.

## Developing class experts

Invite students to nominate experts in a particular learning skill or aspect of your subject. In the spirit of *reflectiveness* and *reciprocity*, the students may nominate themselves or another student within the group who they feel has strengths in this area. You might, as the teacher, choose to decide the most appropriate students to be named as experts for each skill or, for a truly co-constructed learning environment, you may wish to let the students vote for the experts themselves.

Once the experts have been appointed, the class needs to 'ask an expert' before they ask the teacher for help with a particular problem.

You may choose to appoint different students as experts after an appropriate period of time to model *responsiveness* and *reciprocity*.

You may wish to appoint two 'learning monitors' to watch what is going on throughout the lesson and lead the plenary or meta-learning review. They could be asked to answer the following questions, providing reasons for their answers:

- Have all students achieved the learning outcomes for the lesson? If not, why? Which students have achieved the learning outcomes?
- How well have people worked today? Has everybody stayed on task?
- What lessons can we learn from how we have worked today to help us next lesson or next time we undertake a similar learning experience?

## Introducing tools for developing creative thinking

There are a variety of texts that describe methods of developing creative thinking. Below we have headlined the ideas and refer you to the texts to find out more:

1 4Rs: Re-expression, Related worlds, Revolution and Random links. See *Sticky Wisdom: How to Start a Creative Revolution at Work* (Allan et al 2002).

2 De Bono's thinking hats (white hat – facts, figures and information; red hat – emotion, feeling, hunches; black hat – caution, truth, judgement; yellow hat – advantages, benefits; green hat – exploration; blue hat – thinking about thinking). See *Teach Your Child to Think* (De Bono 1993).

3 See *Ideaship: How to Get Ideas Flowing in the Workplace* (Foster 2001) and try to apply the techniques to your classroom, such as: 'don't ask for one solution ask for many'; 'make their jobs seem easy'; 'give them more than one problem at a time'; 'let them shine'; 'share experiences'; 'search for ways to create fun'.

**4** In his book *A Technique for Producing Ideas*, James Webb Young (2003) describes ideas as new combinations, and to generate new ideas he suggests that it is important to work on heightening the ability to see relationships. He proposes a five-step procedure for doing this:

a) gathering all the material;

b) the mental digestive process or working over the materials in your mind;

c) the incubation stage or constantly thinking about it;

d) the birth of the idea;

e) the shaping and development of the idea to its final stage.

This approach is probably akin to that used in art or in design and technology. It may be useful to think about it as a five-stage process, to share it with students and to develop further exploratory and investigative processes to enhance each of the stages described.

Creative thinking is linked to the attitudes of resilience, reflectiveness and resourcefulness. Teachers at Villiers have complained that students latch onto the first idea they come up with and that they find it difficult to get students to explore more and different ideas to widen their interpretation of a theme. If this is your experience, these creative tools may help students to do just this.

## Questioning in a learning-to-learn classroom

Questions are a great way to start any learning experience. They can be used as an abstract starter to help the students focus and to get them thinking. For example, variations on the 'yes–no game' (also sometimes known as the 'Post–it game'; that is, displaying the name of a person or an object somewhere where everybody apart from one person can see it and asking the 'guesser' to work out who or what the information describes by asking a limited number of questions to which the rest of the group are only allowed to reply 'yes' or 'no'. This can, of course, be reversed so that one person knows a piece of information that the rest of the group are trying to find out. This game is very revealing about effective question choice and the power of questions to allow us to eliminate irrelevant knowledge.

Similarly, covering up parts of the views to diagrams, pictures and illustrations and asking students to use questions to work out what they are seeing is a great way to get them thinking. The spotlight tool on interactive whiteboards makes this very easy.

As well as considering strategies to question and challenge students (some or all of them), we also consider how the students might best use questioning as a tool to help them learn more, learn better or become better learners. For example, display the intended learning outcomes at the start of the lesson and allow groups of students five minutes to generate a set of questions to ask you in order to find out exactly what it is they are going to be doing in order to achieve the outcomes.

We have found that encouraging students to ask each other questions helps to develop an ethos of co-operation and *reciprocity* among a group or whole class. In order to encourage and promote this, simply build in three minutes at the start of all paired or group activities in which students ask each other questions about themselves. It may sound trivial, but it can start the groups off on a collaborative note. In addition to this, ensure that there is always a member of each group who uses questions to check that all understand what to do.

A teacher who is committed to the idea of a learning-to-learn classroom and co-constructing the learning experience will use questions in a 'thinking-out loud' way to model the characteristics of effective learners. The teacher might also reflect one student's answer back to another and encourage them to add, develop and critique each other's responses. In this way, the position of the teacher as the asker of questions and hence the font of all knowledge is shifted to a facilitator who guides the students through questioning each other as well as asking the right questions of their teacher. Just as an effective chairperson in a meeting will encourage participation from all members and prevent individuals from monopolising the discussion, an effective teacher will encourage all students to play an active role in both the asking and the answering of questions.

The position of students in the classroom and the layout of the classroom have an impact upon the quality of the questioning and responses given. For more guidance and suggestions about this, please refer to 'Room layout' in 'Creating physical resources' on page 122. It is equally important to consider the positioning of the teacher. All too often the teacher stands at the front of the class during question and answer sessions. This naturally guides all answers through them and can hinder the students' engagement in each other's questioning and thinking. We suggest always taking this into account; for example, during a discussion about an issue-based topic, it is useful for the teacher to organise the class into a circle and to sit among the circle. As each student contributes they must first respond to the ideas or questions of the last speaker before continuing themselves.

Here are some techniques to use to encourage all students to participate in questioning sessions and discussions:

- Put the names of students in a 'hat' and pull out names to decide who will speak.
- Have two packs of cards. Give each student a card and have a second pack. Pick cards to decide who will speak.
- Give each student three tokens and encourage students to spend their tokens by making a contribution to discussion.

# Creating the right atmosphere for learning

In the classroom, it is sometimes difficult for students to put their learning first. This is probably especially true for adolescents where the pressures of being liked, being cool and identifying with a particular group are very strong factors influencing behaviour; so it is important to make the classroom emotionally neutral by getting the right atmosphere for learning.

One way to achieve this is to go through a particular ritual with students when they enter the classroom – this is equivalent to signing a role in a rehearsal room. As they go through the ritual the students can say: 'I am in the classroom and here I put my learning first.' This gives all the students the permission to suspend their out-of-class friendships for the period of the lesson and to resume them as normal when they leave the classroom without causing any ill feeling. It is helpful to use symbols as part of this ritual: an 'L badge', an 'L card' on the desk, or a token. As the students prepare to leave the classroom, they can unsign their learner role in a similar ritual where they say: 'I am leaving the classroom and I am signing off my role as learner.'

# Use of language

The language we use when talking to groups of students and individuals is key to encouraging them to take responsibility. When students ask you questions about what they should do to address an issue or challenge, avoid the immediate temptation to offer a solution. Turn the question back to them and ask them what they think they should do.

When students break school rules or refuse to co-operate, offer them a choice of actions; once they have made a choice, play back their choice to them if necessary, so that they cannot blame you for the consequences.

At Villiers, we have abandoned the term scheme of work and replaced it with schemes of learning, and lesson plans have become learning plans. We try not to use the word 'work' and to replace it with the word 'learning'. These may seem like small matters but we think they are important in creating a good learning ethos.

Good self-esteem plays a significant part in learning (see BBC Worldwide 2004). Using language to help students develop good self-esteem is all part of encouraging good learning. Some tips to do this are:

- Find as many opportunities as possible to praise students in and out of the classroom as groups and as individuals.
- Avoid sarcasm and put-downs.
- Create opportunities to make every student feel special and always avoid comparing one student to another. For example, pass on good comments from other teachers; notice when students make a special effort and congratulate them; send cards home; give students special badges; comment on badges given by other teachers. All these things help students to feel good about school and about themselves.

- Talk with students about the future and not the past. So that when a student has behaved badly emphasise the positive behaviour you would like to see rather than going over the 'bad behaviour'. This is particularly important because if we emphasise the negative, this is what students think of as we say it. If we emphasise the positive, they think of and remember the positive.

For more about language use, see 'Check your Language' in *The Teachers' Toolkit* (Ginnis 2002).

## Involving students in whole-school organisation

In Chapter 12, we describe in some detail our student lesson observer scheme, which has been very successful. In addition to this, there are many other ways in which the students can take responsibility for and ownership of the school organisation. These whole-school opportunities create an atmosphere among the students that encourages maturity and empowers students to accept responsibility for themselves as individuals and learners and for the student community as a whole. All of this contributes to creating a learning-to-learn ethos. Here are some examples of what we do at Villiers:

- A student prefect system set up, run and managed by the students in Years 10 and 11.
- Activities Week led and managed by students in Year 9.
- The international student conference organised by students and staff working together (see www.villiers.ealing.sch.uk).
- Redesigning the school uniform: new design created by students to a clear specification.
- The student year book and 'prom' designed and managed by Year 11 students.
- School magazine designed and created by students.
- An annual fashion show led by a group of students.
- All Key Stage 4 students create their own business and make profits that they keep.
- Students run the school radio station.
- Students generate fund-raising activities for charity, such as selling cakes, blind date.
- Students work with staff to create assemblies – for example, making DVDs; devising role plays, writing poems – and students ask to take assemblies on themes that concern them.
- Students make presentations at staff meetings and training days.
- Students take part in interviews for teachers.
- Students run a recycle, reduce and reuse campaign for the school environment.
- Joint training activities in which students learn with staff at an event facilitated by an external consultant. Recently, we ran a cross-curricular training session with representative staff from all faculties and students from Year 8 and Year 10. Staff learned alongside students.

■ Student behaviour monitors pick up bullying and work together with student juries to implement a system of student justice based on principles of restorative justice.

## Summary

At Villiers, our approach to learning-to-learn has been to introduce the ASK curriculum to teach the attitudes, skills and knowledge of learning-to-learn. However, learning-to-learn is enhanced and strengthened by adopting a range of general strategies and methods in the classroom that shift the focus from the teacher to the learner, from teaching to learning and from completing tasks to learning skills, concepts and processes. We suggest that the approaches we have discussed in this chapter together with the explicit teaching of the ASK curriculum will equip your students with the capabilities and motivation to enjoy learning and to learn effectively without the need for constant intervention by teachers and others. This has to be the ultimate aim for teachers and schools. It is only by achieving this aim that we have truly educated the young people that pass through our schools.

# PART 3

## Putting it all into practice

# Introduction to Part 3

In Parts 1 and 2 we introduced:

- the rationale for learning-to-learn
- the ASK curriculum
- practical ideas for teaching the elements of learning-to-learn.

Now we go beyond the classroom to suggest:

- ways of involving the students in creating an ethos for learning-to-learn
- ideas for staff development
- some of the leadership issues related to developing learning-to-learn across a whole school.

# 12 Learning-to-learn and student leadership

*by Amarjit Garcha*

*'The task of the leader is to get his people from where they are to where they have not been.'*

HENRY KISSINGER

*'To lead people, walk beside them ... When the best leader's work is done the people say, We did it ourselves!'*

LAO-TSU

## COMING UP IN THIS CHAPTER:

▶ Our approach to engaging students.
▶ How we planned and delivered student conferences.
▶ How we developed student lesson observers.

So far in this book, we have concentrated on the development of ASK within lessons. Indeed, we have stressed the importance of learning-to-learn taking place within the classroom and being the responsibility of the subject teacher. As we have already explained, this ensures that relevant sections of attitudes, skills and knowledge can be applied and transferred in different subjects when they are most needed. This model also gives ownership of the learning-to-learn curriculum to teachers and therefore hopefully to their students.

However, learning-to-learn and ASK are bigger than just classroom subjects. An aim of the learning-to-learn curriculum is to develop lifelong learning attitudes, skills and knowledge that are relevant and helpful in all areas of life. This needs to be reflected in the environment around the school and not just in the classroom. A learning-to-learn school continues to encourage and develop its principles and ethos everywhere – from the school canteen to the playground, from the corridors to the changing rooms, from its caretaker to its governors. It leads to a fundamental change in the attitude of the school's population, so that the staffroom is buzzing with positive 'learnacy' talk and everywhere there are 'learnatic' students actively seeking to extend their experiences.

There will come a time when students who have been taught a more learning-orientated curriculum will naturally need to 'try out' some of the new knowledge they have. The school will also understandably want to find ways to see the impact that learning-to-learn is having on the students and how they cope in different situations and challenges.

In addition to this, there are, as would be expected, some students who develop faster and master their new learning-focused curriculum more quickly. They

**133**

are not necessarily the more able students, but are often those who have already developed fairly sophisticated approaches to coping with the demands of studying many different subjects and making progress in most areas without necessarily being consciously aware of the skills they are using. We found early on that each class had one or two students who naturally seemed to take to learning-to-learn and quickly developed a learning vocabulary.

It was for these reasons that we began to discuss the creation of a leadership team of students for learning-to-learn. A leadership team was an appealing idea, not only to find ways of taking manageable numbers of learning-to-learn students outside the classroom, but also to find ways of stretching the knowledge and experiences of the few really talented students in this area. These students also offered a powerful insight into what was happening in different learning-to-learn lessons. Like the student lesson observers, discussed later in this section, they provided essential information about classroom practice from a student perspective.

There are many ways of choosing students to play leadership roles within school and different schools have their own models. We simply asked form tutors to collect feedback from teachers about students' learning-to-learn performances during lessons. The same names cropped up in many subjects and we quickly built up a picture of students who were ahead of the majority of their peers. We spoke informally and formally to all nominated students and assessed their enthusiasm and vision for learning-to-learn. We decided upon having two 'leaders' in each form group. The students selected were invited to an initial meeting and were asked what they thought the potential was of having student leaders for learning-to-learn. As you might expect from any group of hand-selected students, they were very enthusiastic!

The team now has, over the course of each academic year, the following responsibilities: the production of whole-school and year-group assemblies; the dissemination of learning-to-learn developments to their peers during tutorial time; leadership of Year 6 students at learning-to-learn student conferences; monitoring the regular teaching of learning-to-learn in subject areas; participation in reflection and evaluation sessions for the development of the learning-to-learn curriculum in the future; and many are student lesson observers.

These students are as instrumental and important to the development of learning-to-learn at Villiers as any subject or cross-curricular group with a responsibility for learning-to-learn. The next two chapters illustrate in detail some of the ways these young leaders are able to use and develop their learning-to-learn attitudes, skills and knowledge.

## Learning-to-learn student conferences

'I know things you don't, and the other way round. I can do some things better than you, but other things you can help me with. We all lead sometimes.'

Fardowsa Ali, Year 8

The status of any leadership role in school is important and as learning-to-learn is the major teaching and learning initiative at Villiers, we decided that the standing and value of what we offered our new leaders should reflect the importance of their role. It was at this point that we decided to hold a two-day learning-to-learn conference and to send formal invitations to our student leaders.

As well as continuing to develop our leaders, we wanted them to experience learning challenges in a very real way that is not always possible in the classroom. In an attempt to give them genuine leadership responsibility for the learning of others, we decided to invite Year 6 students from local primary schools as delegates to the conference.

As this book goes to print, we have successfully run two learning-to-learn conferences – the last with 96 delegates – and are planning the third. What follows is hopefully an interesting and useful description of the key parts and elements of the conferences, as well as their aims and intended outcomes. Although some of what is described below may seem common sense, its inclusion is to highlight areas that are often overlooked in the planning and running of school events. It also shows the importance of working with as many areas of school staff as possible, from teachers to canteen staff. A successful cross-curricular event requires input from a variety of staff and the support of the whole school.

## Approaching and running an event at school

You will be all too aware that the outcomes of an event that takes students off timetable has to justify taking students out of lessons. It is helpful if staff see it is linked to what they are doing in their classrooms. With this in mind, we have found it useful to invite all teachers to contribute ideas for the conferences. Recognising how busy teachers can be, we created a planning group of teachers experienced in teaching learning-to-learn to take part in preparation for the conference.

It is accepted that the conditions in which people learn are extremely important and a pre-planned event can be a great opportunity to try to create the perfect environment for learning to take place.

We chose our rooms to accommodate the needs of what we planned – workshops, presentations, guest speakers and other activities. The layout of each was carefully thought through involving and consulting the ICT department to ensure that everything was resourced using all available technology – smartboards, projectors, audio/visual devices, filming and other digital media.

Student delegates are no different to adult delegates and we all know how important the food is on an INSET day or outside training course. We wanted our students to work really hard, and we recognised that this is an energetic business. We worked closely with the schools' caterers to provide a first-class lunch for the students at both of our conferences: full of choice, everything nutritional and appetising. The lunch was extremely well received and is still discussed by the students as a real highlight. We also trialled a working, 'sandwich/buffet-style lunch' for the last day of the second conference.

The key decision that ensured success was to separate the conference breaks and lunchtime from the normal break times, to avoid the business of the rest of the school. We wanted the students to feel refreshed by their breaks, able to reflect and discuss what they were doing and come back to the sessions ready to continue learning.

Finally, to help the student leaders to value their role we wanted them to feel excited by the possibilities of their work and to be aware of its importance to the school. To this end we gave them plenty of information in advance and involved parents and carers in the process as much as possible. Writing letters home formally inviting the students to events raised the status of what they were doing. Organising meetings beforehand to share our aims and objectives helped to ensure that students understood the expectations and purpose of the event. We spent a long time designing the welcome packs for student delegates, both in the design of the cover and in its contents. We chose relevant reading material to help the students prepare for the conference and made sure that detailed programmes were included with as much information about the timings of the events as possible. It was a lot of work, but the look of pride on the faces of the students as they clutched their folders and kept them safe made us sure that it had been worth it.

As far as we are aware our approach to planning and running the student conferences has been no different to our approach to planning and running learning-to-learn INSET days for staff at Villiers and this seems the truest interpretation of the aims of learning-to-learn possible.

# Learning-to-learn student conference 1

The first conference was attended by 56 delegates in total – mainly from Year 6 and Year 7, with a small number of Year 8 and Year 9 students who were there to find out about learning-to-learn in Year 7 and to consider ways to build it into their own learning experiences after the conference.

We decided early on that the conference should be designed to explore new knowledge about learning and how the brain learns. We also wanted to give students opportunities to develop their skills in key areas of the ASK curriculum and to explore the importance of having the right attitude to learning.

To fulfil these aims we fixed upon the idea of delivering the theory about learning through quite formal presentations and talks at key times during the conference. We then ran a carousel of workshops, each focusing on developing a particular attitude and skill, giving the students opportunities to personalise the theory and try it out in a variety of settings and activities. We planned that the groups would rotate around the workshops until each group had attended all four. The workshops were run by two teachers from the learning-to-learn team at Villiers. They made every effort to plan stimulating and challenging sessions, which explored their chosen area of ASK in creative ways.

Additionally, we wanted to challenge students' ideas about learning and their own understanding of how they learn and how they can help others learn. It was important to build in a time when students checked their understanding of the ASK curriculum they were covering. To cater for this, we structured student-led sessions into the second day after the main activities, but before the Learning Trail.

We gave groups of four the task of developing teaching and learning resources that would help their teachers and peers develop some of the attitudes, skills and knowledge that they been focusing on at the conference.

Students chose to produce the following:

- PowerPoint presentations giving theory and information about particular attitudes or skills.
- Short films in which presenters gave theory and information about particular attitudes or skills and set tasks to the viewer.
- Board games and other games testing players' learning skills and knowledge.
- Assemblies designed to inform audiences about the learning-to-learn conference at Villiers and what students had learned – including PowerPoint presentations.
- Short drama productions (plays) about the importance of having the right attitude to learn effectively.

Copies of all work was collected and used by the students to disseminate and share their experiences of the conferences.

Finally, we wanted the students to enjoy learning in a variety of ways and in particular for the conference to end on a really memorable high. For this reason, we planned and ran a Learning Trail. Essentially, this is a series of fun activities designed to challenge students' thinking skills and their reciprocity. The Learning Trail, as it became known, was loosely based on the TV show *The Crystal Maze*.

In groups of four, students were given an hour to visit and complete ten different challenges, all in different areas of the school. Once they were at an activity place, they had to read the information about the challenge on the door and decide which two team members would attempt the challenge; the remaining two team members were asked to sit out. If the active pair successfully completed the challenge, the team would earn two learning stickers. The key to success was for group members to share their skills and to know who to choose for each challenge; for example, if a student felt their strengths did not lie in code-cracking numbers, then they should opt out of the 'number walk'. At the end of the Learning Trail, each team's stickers were added up and a winning team was declared and presented with an award.

The key skills being tested by the Learning Trail were: approaching a task, problem solving, asking questions, managing group dynamics, time management, planning, learning from mistakes, and understanding of self as learner.

The Learning Trail was probably the most labour-intensive part of the planning process and needed a lot of monitoring on the day. However, it was also the most energetic part of the conference and students still talk about the excitement of it today!

## Learning-to-learn student conference 2

The second conference was attended by 96 students, including 20 Year 8 students, 20 Year 7 students and 48 students from six local primary schools. There were also eight Year 9 students in role as characters from the 'Whodunnit'.

The main difference between this and the first student conference was taking into account the student delegates from Year 8 who had already participated in one conference and who had been taught attitudes, skills and knowledge from the ASK curriculum throughout Year 7.

We wanted the structure of the conference to allow more input and control from the student delegates. Rather than the previous structure of talks and workshops, we worked on developing a longer role-play exercise that would allow the students to use their attitudes, skills and knowledge from ASK as they worked on something real. After trial planning a few ideas, including a Greenpeace conference and a local council budget meeting, we set upon the idea of a 'Whodunnit' because of its popular appeal and the variety of areas of ASK that would be involved in solving a crime. The investigation was planned to last the whole of the first day and a part of the second and student delegates were to work as part of an investigation team trying to solve the crime. A crime scene was designed for the school stage and the school hall was laid out as an enormous investigation room. Information and clues about the crime were to be introduced to the investigation teams as and when they asked questions and made choices and decisions.

We decided that the important learning-to-learn theory would still be presented to the students formally, but that it would come in the form of talks given during the 'on-going investigation' and would be planned to come at times that meant that its focus would be relevant and helpful to the investigation. The theory could therefore be tried out in practice straight afterwards and have a greater chance of being developed and remembered. For example, just before we allowed groups to choose which suspects to interview, we planned a presentation by a guest speaker about effective questioning and its place in thinking. Similarly, we planned a 'good presentation workshop' just before the students had to prepare their presentation about the decisions they had made about who to arrest.

The 'Whodunnit' itself was developed with the help of the English department and was based on a unit of work that already existed. We organised a crime scene and invited the local community police officer to join us and introduce the role-play, to give it more interest and authenticity.

After the 'Whodunnit' was over, we wanted to consolidate the learning-to-learn elements of the conference and planned a student-led session in which small groups were asked to prepare presentations with the purpose of informing their peers about the learning-to-learn student conference. For this we used the ICT suites and saved all the presentations for the students to receive their own copy and for the school to keep as a record of their work and thinking.

Finally, the conference ended with a Learning Trail similar to the one run at the end of the first conference. The increase in numbers meant that each activity needed to be run twice simultaneously, but it still proved to be as motivating and successful as the first Learning Trail, again ending the conference on an energetic and enthusiastic note.

## Ensuring more challenge for Year 8 students

The Year 8 delegates had had learning-to-learn as part of their curriculum for over a year by the time of the second student conference. While we still felt that they would benefit from taking part in the conference, we also felt that this was a good opportunity for them to test some of their new skills and knowledge in real situations and to evaluate their performances. It was important to differentiate the conference so that they were being stretched in their learning knowledge. The conference was a good opportunity to assess the impact of ASK on their ability to perform in a learning environment.

It was therefore decided that as well as being members of the detective teams, Year 8 students would be given the extra responsibility of being the leader of each group and to have leadership responsibilities to make sure the groups functioned well. This meant that, at times, they would have to separate themselves from the investigation to make decisions about how best to run the group. In order that they were prepared for their roles, we ran some training and discussion sessions with them and also explained that they would be evaluating their performances and learning-to-learn abilities after the conference.

Interestingly, in the sessions before the conference the Year 8 students were very confident about being successful in their dual role as both delegates and learning-to-learn leaders. They could not see how or why it would be in any way difficult to run or manage the groups based on the attitudes, skills and knowledge they had developed so far through ASK at Villiers. However, it was apparent very early on, that most of the Year 8 students were so keen on solving the murder mystery and enjoying themselves at the conference that they quickly forgot their leadership roles and, despite frequent reminders, were unable to manage and guide their groups on any effective level. Those students that did try to offer leadership to their groups at times, reported later that they found the 'language and action' required in leadership to be very demanding and much more difficult than they had anticipated. Indeed, the evaluation of the conference with Year 8 proved a very valuable experience as it highlighted the importance of trying out learning-to-learn in real settings, in order to apply theory and new learning, as an essential part of the learning process. What often seems straightforward in theory can be remarkably difficult in practice, especially when the practice involves real-life settings with real people involved – as it nearly always does!

---

## TIPS FOR RUNNING A SUCCESSFUL LEARNING-TO-LEARN EVENT

- Create a team of experienced and enthusiastic learning-to-learn teachers to help plan the conference.
- Carefully plan every detail, from the content of the theory to the time and menu of the lunch.
- Keep other teachers informed and involved as much as possible.
- Ensure that the students value their role and involvement and make them feel important and special.
- Share your aims and objectives with the student delegates.
- Bring the beliefs of learning-to-learn into all aspects of the event.
- Make sure the activities, resources and contents of the event are challenging and engaging.

---

## Involving students as student lesson observers

A successful learning-to-learn programme will raise questions about the opportunities offered to students to get involved in influencing the teaching and learning they experience at school. Students who have a clearer understanding of themselves as learners will, quite naturally, begin to have opinions about how best they and others learn. This has the potential to provide the starting point for the creation of a genuinely collaborative approach between teachers and students.

Delivering the ASK curriculum at Villiers has made us look more closely at the possibilities of such a partnership and one of the outcomes of this has been the creation of student lesson observers.

Mastering teaching, like mastering any skill, involves being critical and learning from mistakes. Teachers own reflective practice is therefore vital to enhance classroom practice. In recognition of this, we have for some time been establishing a culture of frequent lesson observation, team-planning, team-teaching and team-coaching as part of our regular practice. However, up until this time our students had been excluded from the process.

Schools, including ours, are constantly searching for ways to make improvements for their students, but how often do they use students to give specific feedback on teaching despite the fact that students are well placed to highlight areas of concern that may have gone unnoticed and to come up with suggestions for improvement.

A true learning-to-learn school is one where the principles of learning-to-learn run throughout as many areas of school life as possible, and bringing students into the planning of lessons and listening to and learning from their feedback about teaching and learning is an obvious way to do this.

# Developing a team of student observers

For us the first vital step was to ensure the support of teachers. As a school, we are very lucky to have an ethos where professional development has been and remains highly valued, which made embarking on this new project much easier and many staff volunteered to become involved.

We began with brainstorming the advantages that student lesson observers would bring and any concerns for both the students and the teachers, keeping in mind the ethos and environment we wished to develop. We summarised our thoughts under the following four sections: benefits to the school, benefits to the teachers, benefits to the students and any concerns.

Benefits to the school:

- Engage students in school life
- Increase student participation
- Promote confidence and self-esteem
- Learn/develop the skills base
- Enhance achievement
- Offer more responsibility
- Improve quality of teaching and learning
- Generate a collaborative ethos
- More effective delivery of learning-to-learn
- Dissemination of good practice
- Positive impact on behaviour.

Benefit to the teachers:

- Support for teachers (more appreciation of their work by students)
- More ideas to improve quality of teaching
- Better understanding of students' perspective
- More student involvement in every stage of teaching
- Better understanding of teacher's 'job'.

Benefits for the students:

- Feeling of inclusion and contribution to the school (a student voice)
- Seeing teaching and learning from a new dimension
- Feeling responsible for their own learning
- Empowering them to influence their own learning
- Making them more reflective in their thinking
- Identifying basic features of good lessons, such as explicit objectives, starter
- Learn about learning.

Concerns that may arise:

- Some students are too passive (not articulate enough to give effective feedback)
- Trust between observers/teachers observed
- Threat of being checked
- Threat of being criticised – decreasing the teacher's self-esteem
- Ethos shift.

Clearly the pros of the project heavily outweighed the cons and we felt that over time and with our commitment, any concerns could be overcome in a positive way.

Our first step for the implementation of student lesson observers was to see this in practice at another school. We had heard that the Matthew Moss School in Rochdale had established a student observers' programme already. The headteacher, Andy Raymer, and his deputies arranged for us to sit in on some lessons, and then watch while students gave their feedback. We were given time to sit with the student observers as they reflected on the observed lesson and as they gave feedback. Impressed with what we had seen, we came back determined to embrace this venture wholeheartedly at Villiers.

The next day, inspired by the findings from Matthew Moss School, we began our careful preparation to get the staff on board. We knew that good development of the groundwork was key to the success of the project and this meant drawing up an action plan with clear targets. We have found that the initial success of new initiatives at school can very much depend upon the personal understanding and involvement of teachers. We all know how busy the school day is and it is often the case that emails can be read, but not fully absorbed.

With this in mind we decided to visit and talk, on an individual and informal basis, to as many of the staff as possible about the student lesson observers over the next few days, giving them information and opportunities to ask questions, so that any concerns they had were answered before we presented formally to the staff. This was very time-consuming, but proved to be worthwhile as, within a week, when we presented our ideas and thoughts to the whole staff, teachers were overwhelmingly supportive of our proposals and plan of implementation. This meant we were in a position to proceed – with their support giving us a massive boost to go ahead. We next shifted our attention to the students' roles. We had already made a joint decision that we wanted to start with the Year 7 students, as they had experienced the learning-to-learn curriculum and, as a result, had a greater understanding of teaching and learning.

We approached the students through a year assembly and visited form groups. All the students were given explanatory letters and the application forms (see Figures 12.1 and 12.2). Over the next few days, we had a huge response with over 80 returned application forms! Short-listing followed promptly and interviews with a panel of two teachers and two student council representatives for each applicant were arranged (see Figure 12.3). The responses to the interview questions offered us a good insight into each student's capability and potential, and we finally selected a group of 20.

Dear Student

The teachers at Villiers are constantly working on improving the quality of lessons. They do this by planning lessons together, watching each other teach and having special training. The reason for this is that we want to give our students the best learning experience that we can.

We think that the next step towards getting even better would be to involve our students in helping us to evaluate lessons and tell us what works well and what could be done differently to help students to learn more effectively. We would really like to develop a partnership with students whereby we work together (teachers and students) to create the best lessons we can.

We think students can help us to work out the best teaching approaches and we also think that students will become better learners if they are involved in working with teachers to create really good lessons. We think that if students work in partnership with teachers they will benefit because they will take an equal responsibility for their own learning along with the teacher.

We have decided to invite Year 7 students to volunteer to become lesson observers. Those interested will have to apply and prove that they can do this. Those who are selected will be trained over a period of two days. Once trained they will watch about three lessons in one term and discuss them with the teacher.

If you are interested in becoming a student observer, you will need to complete an application form and return it to me on Wednesday 13 July. Those applicants who are short-listed will be interviewed.

I hope you are interested in this. I look forward to receiving your application

Thank you

Mrs A. Garcha

**Figure 12.1**

---

If you would like to apply to be a Student Lesson Observer, please fill out this form and hand it into your Form Tutor by Wednesday 13 July 2005.

Personal Details:
Name: ................................................................ Form: ................................................................

1    From the words and phrases below, choose **five** that you feel are your main strengths *(please circle the five words you choose)*.

| | | | | |
|---|---|---|---|---|
| Good listener | punctual | organised | quick thinker | creative |
| Good leader | positive | inspirational | clear communicator | |
| Reflective | Resilient | Reciprocal | Responsive | |
| Responsible | confident speaker | team player | Resourceful | |

2    How would you describe your attendance?

    ................................................................................................................................................

3    List **three** things that you think makes a good lesson.
    a) ............................................................................................................................................
    b) ............................................................................................................................................
    c) ............................................................................................................................................

4    Briefly describe why you would make a good student lesson observer *(no more than 50 words)*.

    ................................................................................................................................................

    ................................................................................................................................................

**Figure 12.2**

---

**Interview questions**

1 Tell us about a lesson that you thought was excellent and explain why it was such a good lesson.

2 Look at the words you have circled on your application form and describe how you have used two of the strengths you have highlighted.

3 Tell us about a positive contribution you have made to Villiers High School in Year 7 so far.

4 How do you think having Student Lesson Observers will benefit Villiers High School?

5 An English teacher teaches a private reading lesson in their classroom and makes the students read silently for one hour. Can you give us some ideas of the feedback that you would give to that teacher afterwards?

6 Do you have any questions you would like to ask us?

---

**Figure 12.3**

Soon afterwards we ran a two–day intensive training programme for these students. Our aim was to have an immediate impact on the students. We agreed that this meant involving students in a series of team-building exercises followed by a strong introduction from a well-spoken outsider. Our training was initiated with a superb presentation to engage all the students and there was a great emphasis on how lucky they were to be given this opportunity. With this strong beginning, we moved onto a short series of sessions that involved students devising and discussing, 'What makes a good lesson?' Various recorded lessons were seen, and students were given an understanding of the vocabulary and the different constituents of lessons. The initial feedback resulted in the broad categories that they developed further into a model of an excellent lesson.

· · · · · · · · · · · · · · · · · · · · · · · · · · · · · · · · · · · · · · · · · · · · · · · · · · · · ·

# Model of an excellent lesson

### Devised by student observers

Teacher is punctual.

Brings in the class quietly.

Students engage in linking objectives to previous learning.

Teacher tries to find out about prior knowledge and/or experience.

The teacher explains what is going to happen in the lesson (objectives) – related to subject and learning-to-learn.

Teacher is prepared for the lesson and explains the tasks fully.

Students of different abilities are catered for (differentiation).

The class is kept involved, entertained, interested and active and encouraged to be resourceful, resilient, reciprocal and responsive.

There are different activities for students to do such as practical work, reading and writing and so on.

There is a balance of these activities.

Students are encouraged to ask questions.

There is a chance for students to learn with and from others.

There is an encouragement for students to do 'thinking' and be resilient.

Half of the lesson time is for teacher activities and half for student activities.

Class is controlled in the lesson.

Teacher goes around and asks students questions to see if they are learning.

Checking learning is done several times in the lesson in different ways.

There is an opportunity for students to be reflective in their own learning.

Class is dismissed in an orderly way.

● ● ● ● ● ● ● ● ● ● ● ● ● ● ● ● ● ● ● ● ● ● ● ● ● ● ● ● ● ● ● ● ● ● ● ● ● ● ● ● ● ● ● ● ● ● ● ● ● ● ● ● ●

With the vital components of a good lesson fresh in students' minds, we moved onto the next activity. Students were split into five groups and asked to draw up a lesson observation form that they would use during practice lesson observations on the following day. Different formats were produced and each group presented their version – finally the group made the decision to choose the version shown in Figure 12.4.

The second day of training was designed to apply what the students had been learning. We started with some team-building exercises and this was followed by watching a 15-minute lesson on DVD, with students using their lesson observation materials from the day before. In groups of four, they brainstormed the feedback that could be offered. We asked two groups to role-play their feedback and this became the basis of discussion of how feedback should be given and what it should include.

For the final part of the training, students in pairs/threes, accompanied by one trainer sat in on 'real' lessons. On returning from the live observations there was little time to catch up with how the students felt in this new role because feedback had to be prepared and given within the hour, and the students were determined to give the best they could. There was nervousness but there was also excitement and a sense of achievement to have come so far.

## Lesson observation checklist

| Teacher | Period | Subject |
|---------|--------|---------|
| Class | Date | Topic |

Shade in the boxes

### What I saw and heard: Learning

| Were the subject objectives made clear? |
|---|
| Not at all |
| Totally |

| Were the L to L objectives made clear? |
|---|
| Not at all |
| Totally |

| Was subject learning checked? |
|---|
| Never |
| Throughout |

| Were L to L outcomes checked? |
|---|
| Never |
| Throughout |

Suggestion box

### What I saw and heard: Students

| How involved were students? |
|---|
| Not at all |
| Completely |

| Were the activities suitable? |
|---|
| Not at all |
| Completely |

| Was there enough variety? (VAK) |
|---|
| Very little |
| Lots |

| Were students given opportunities to ask questions? |
|---|
| Not at all |
| Throughout |

| Was prior knowledge and experience acknowledged? |
|---|
| A little |
| Lots |

| Was the work adequate for all students? |
|---|
| Partly |
| Totally |

| Were the students encouraged to think? |
|---|
| Partly |
| Totally |

| Were the students given a chance to have their say? |
|---|
| Hardly |
| Totally |

Suggestion box

**Figure 12.4**

| What I saw and heard: Teacher | |
|---|---|
| | How well did the teacher manage the class?<br>World's best<br>World's worst |
| | How did the teacher come across?<br>Very poorly<br>Very well |
| | How prepared and organised was the teacher<br>0%<br>100% |
| | How many of the students did the teacher manage to involve?<br>None<br>All |
| | How was the lesson put together? (structure)<br>Very poorly<br>Well |

Suggestion box

| What I saw and heard: Attitudes | |
|---|---|
| | Was Responsiveness developed?<br>No<br>A lot |
| | Was Resourcefulness developed?<br>No<br>A lot |
| | Was Resilience developed?<br>No<br>A lot |
| | Was Reciprocity developed?<br>No<br>A lot |
| | Was Reflection developed?<br>No<br>A lot |

Suggestion box

| What I saw and heard: Checking progress | |
|---|---|
| | How much progress was made by the class?<br>Very little<br>Loads |

Suggestion box

**Figure 12.4 cont.**

147

Our training ended with just enough time to discuss and share experiences and plan the next steps. Various areas of concern soon became apparent:

- The students needed more time to prepare and rehearse giving feedback.
- Amendments had to be made to the observation form – in the first instance, all the observations needed to be recorded on blank paper and then transposed onto the observation checklist.
- Teachers needed to support the students in the first term to notice more points in the lesson observation and to deliver feedback.
- It was necessary for some of the main elements in the lessons to be clarified; for example, assessment, checking learning and differentiation.

We implemented the programme of observations in September in the next academic year, after another half-day refresher training session. To start with, each pair of student observers was accompanied by one of the three original trainers, but the lead was taken by the student observers both in observations and feedback sessions.

An example of feedback given by two observers, Gurnoor and Sandeep, for one of the many observed lessons is provided below as a transcript of a students' feedback notes given after observing an English lesson with learning-to-learn objectives.

Gurnoor   Thank you for allowing us to observe your lesson.

Sandeep   How do you think your lesson went?

Gurnoor   We thought your lesson was really fun and students learned a lot from it. It had lots of very good tasks which made it exciting to watch.

Sandeep   We are going to give you the feedback into two parts – first, our positive thoughts, and then areas of development.

Gurnoor   The beginning of the lesson started really well because you explained the subject and the learning-to-learn objectives clearly. You also gave them estimated times for each activity so they could reach each of the objectives and this encouraged the students to take out the equipment they needed to start the lesson quickly.

Sandeep   I thought it was a good idea to ask a lot of questions; for example, 'What was the chapter about?' and 'Why did the author do this?' This meant a lot of students took part in answering and it got their minds thinking about their work. You also gave a few seconds in silence for them to plan their answers and this kept the class quiet.

Gurnoor   Using the interactive whiteboard was a good idea – it was visual for the students. You used this for a few phrases from the book and asked different students to pick out the describing words which helped them with their next task and involved them fully.

Sandeep    I think you were very well organised for the lesson because you had the books, poster paper, colouring pencils and so on before the students came into the class and you had also prepared the work on the interactive board – like the objectives and instructions and this helped the students not to lose time in the lesson.

Gurnoor    You also had a variety of timed activities such as reading, drawing of the character that students were imagining and presenting to the others in the group and the students kept to the time that you had given them.

Sandeep    I liked your idea of not giving the students the answers to the questions they were asking but getting them to find the meaning themselves. This made them look in the dictionary and note the words.

Sandeep    Is there anything that you feel you want to add to the positive points we have given you?

Gurnoor    Do you mind if we give a few suggestions about your lesson?

Sandeep    I think you could have thought about the way that students were working with others. There was one group of students that were not really doing much and they only got the first objective done because only one person was doing the work, the other two were talking.

Gurnoor    Maybe an interactive starter at the beginning of the lesson would get the students thinking straight away as some of the class were not 'fully awake' to start the lesson. You could have done a quick quiz.

Sandeep    Perhaps you could have asked students to think about some questions after they had watched the presentation of each person in their group.

Gurnoor    At the end of the lesson you could have used a way to sum up the work and check if the objectives were reached; for example, using traffic light cards or the thumb-o-meter to check how much progress was made by the students or asked questions and see who got them right and then let that student out.

Gurnoor    Is there anything you would like to add to that?

Sandeep    What do you think of our feedback and can you think of any ways that we could improve it?

## Teachers' views about student observers

To date, 35 staff have volunteered to be observed and our team of 20 observers have carried out 33 observations. Here are some comments from teachers about their role.

'Having had my lesson observed by the student observers, I noted they were polite, punctual, focused throughout both the lesson observation and de-brief and mature in attitude. They had a clear understanding of what they were looking for and felt confident to circulate and talk to the students being taught at the appropriate times during the lesson.

The feedback was given the same day and the student observers had detailed notes of positive comments and ways to develop the lesson further.

Overall, the voice of the student observer scheme is a positive experience for all, especially the students. It allows them to take an additional role in teaching and learning in our school, as well as giving them a greater understanding of both.'

*Amanda Sara*, English teacher

'I have always had the school SLT members, my line manager or other professionals observing me in different lessons. But this time, I had a different feeling when I was being observed by those who were my students in Year 7. Having learned the relevant skills to observe teachers, I felt the student observers could proudly give feedback and express their views and make comments regarding my teaching quality in the lessons. They were very professional and gave me a lot to think about. They restored my confidence by commenting positively in the things I was doing well and gave me strategies that I am keen to give a go! I would have them observing me again!'

*Dan Kia*, ICT teacher

'The two student observers that gave feedback were both pleasant and courteous. Their observations were very useful and it was helpful to consider views from a student's perspective. Equally, I think they gained valuable insights into the teacher's role and it enabled them to consider the job from our perspective.

Meeting to exchange ideas in such a structured framework can only help to foster positive relationships between students and staff and help to develop more mature and responsible attitudes.'

*Marie Hinkson*, science teacher

## Student observers' views

'It helps the school's learning system to get better and also helps teachers with their teaching methods because when I am giving feedback to the teacher it helps them to try out new ideas.'

'It helps us to give our views on the lessons and so teachers will know what we enjoy in them.'

'We learn a lot of new skills and this is going to make us become confident to carry on learning when we leave school. For the teachers, it helps them to think about their lessons more because they take our feedback seriously.'

'We are helping children to learn and achieve their best because the teaching is going to get better.'

'Observing lessons makes us reflective and better learners and we also get a high status in school.'

## Looking to the future

Once every fortnight we all meet at lunchtime and have elected from the student observers a chairperson, secretary and a link person to email staff about the good practices that students are observing in various lessons. Our role as trainers now is to oversee that the project stays on track. Our emphasis throughout has been to ensure anonymity of teachers' observations. The feedback has also been designed in this way and only the teachers observed are privy to the feedback. We feel at Villiers that this feedback is an addition to a teacher's own reflective practice and enables them to continue to develop.

At Villiers, our scheme is still in its infancy. We want to empower many more students in different areas of the school to share their opinions and ideas in a responsible and a reflective manner in partnership with all stakeholders; for example, greater involvement in the school council, the governing body, in a teaching and learning forum and enhancing the role of prefects.

As students leave us to go onto further education it is imperative that they are all equipped with the skills necessary to make their next milestone a success. Nothing can give us greater pleasure as teachers than seeing that we made a difference.

# 13 The INSET implications

*'You must be the change you want to see in the world.'*

MAHATMA GANDHI

## COMING UP IN THIS CHAPTER

▶ A description of effective INSET for learning-to-learn at Villiers High School.
▶ Tips for effective inset.
▶ Examples of INSET programmes for school training days.

When a random selection of our teaching staff were asked the question, 'What features of INSET at Villiers do you find particularly beneficial?', their answers included the following:

'For me, one of Villiers' many strengths are the in-house INSET days. They allow us, the staff: to observe; partake in valuable live lessons; liaise and collaborate with colleagues in planning; learn from experts to enhance professional skills to raise standards of teaching and learning in the classroom. Furthermore, they allow for the development of a shared understanding between ourselves, the Villiers staff, who are working towards a shared vision.'

'The varied nature of what staff will do. There is a nice balance between listening to an expert (whether a guest speaker or one of our colleagues) and then being given the opportunity to put the new skills we have learned into practice. In other words, there is a good balance between theory and practice.'

'I appreciate being offered practical strategies which we can transfer directly to enhance our practice in the classroom.'

'It is good to have the opportunity to share ideas and work together with colleagues from other subject areas.'

'It is nice not to have to teach and to have a good curry for lunch.'

# Whole-staff training days and conferences

We have deliberately involved as many staff as practically possible (typically between five and fifteen) in the organisation, planning and delivery of whole-staff training. This models and reflects one of the defining principles of ASK: giving the learners more responsibility for their own learning as well as providing a valuable professional development opportunity for the staff who have agreed to take part. Other benefits of this approach include giving staff more ownership of ASK, adding variety and interest by having different presenters and more staff becoming 'specialist' in particular areas of ASK. Accordingly, they are more likely to become the 'first port of call' for a teacher with questions about how to teach that particular skill, thereby creating a cross-curricular support network.

A second key ingredient that many staff have found to their benefit is the inclusion in the INSET programme of shared planning and teaching of 'live' lessons. When properly organised, this is a far more powerful professional development tool than, for example, watching a DVD or video footage of a lesson being taught. It is significantly more engaging and interesting because of being real and immediate. The teachers observing know that the lesson has not been 'staged' and that the techniques and strategies they are observing are relevant to their students and their own particular school context.

The inclusion of live lessons as a training tool also provides a good opportunity for the leadership of the school, both at senior leadership level and departmental level, to model key principles and attitudes of learning-to-learn: not least the *reciprocity* and *resourcefulness* involved in collaboratively planning and delivering a varied and engaging lesson. It facilitates quality control as well as providing an excellent forum for *pace-setting leadership* (one of the six Hay-McBer Leadership styles identified by the National College for School Leadership) also known as 'walking the talk'. An additional benefit of collaborative planning followed by actually teaching what has just been planned to a real group of students is that it helps focus the planning sharply on what constitutes an engaging, challenging and worthwhile learning experience. The fact that those planning will also have to teach their plan while being observed by their colleagues prevents the planning part of the exercise from becoming dull and half-hearted.

Third, we have consciously structured opportunities for discussion, reflection, sharing of ideas and collaborative planning among staff from different curriculum subject areas. The motivation for this was to help teachers to see (and later model with their students) how a particular ASK skill or piece of knowledge fits into the 'bigger picture'. This approach has also helped teachers to 'signpost' the transferability of a particular component of ASK to other areas of the curriculum as well as beyond the school environment. Furthermore, a foundation is created for future cross-curricular collaborative work.

The final key feature of our INSET is the distribution of pre-reading material and preparatory work to all the staff taking part several days beforehand. As well as meaning that those participating are not 'going in cold' and meeting concepts and strategies for the very first time, this approach also provides a useful means of setting the necessary background, theoretical context or academic framework in advance. This may provide an additional rationale and add increased depth for the INSET and crucially it frees up time on the day itself to focus on the more practical and 'hands-on' aspects that teachers can adopt directly to enhance their own classroom practice. (For a suggested outline programme of whole-school INSET, see Figure 13.2.)

## Including current models in INSET

According to Stephen Covey in *The Seven Habits of Highly Effective People* (1989), in order to effect any change, three factors must be present: knowledge (knowing *what* to do and *why*); skills (knowing *how* to do it); and, crucially, desire (to *want* to do it).

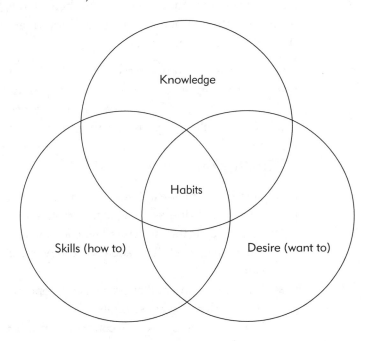

**Figure 13.1 Adapted from Covey (1989)**

In requiring all teachers not only to teach their specialist curriculum subject but also to teach students explicitly how to learn via ASK, clearly we are extending and redefining the role of the teacher. It may be helpful to consider this new definition of what constitutes effective classroom practice by referring to Guy Claxton's four levels of 'proficiency' regarding learning-to-learn:

Level Three   Out of school as well as within
Level Two     Become better learners
Level One     Learn better
Level Zero     Learn more

Level Zero sees the role of the teacher as a 'deliverer of content' with Level One being based on the assumption that if the teacher teaches better (an awareness of different learning styles and consequently a variety of engaging learning activities), then the students will learn better. The aim of ASK and learning-to-learn is to move from Level One to Level Two with the long-term aim of moving students to lifelong learning beyond the classroom (Level Three). Level Two emphasises the need for the student to be given more *responsibility* for their own learning and the teacher to act as a facilitator in this process (for more details, see Claxton 2003). Such a significant change will obviously not be realised without considerable time and thought being given to training all staff to teach ASK effectively.

As well as using the INSET to develop models and practical examples for delivering the various components of ASK, perhaps the most significant aim for this training is to inspire and motivate all staff to change their own perceptions of their role: to see themselves, in the first instance, as teachers of learning and, second, as specialists in their own field and thereby an important *resource* for their students to use to develop their own skills and knowledge in that particular subject area.

To mirror the inter-connected and multi-dimensional nature of ASK and learning-to-learn in general, it seemed appropriate to approach the training of staff in a variety of different formats. Those aspects other than whole-staff INSET days will be explored further in the next chapter.

---

## Tips for effective ASK INSET

■ Significant whole-staff training time is needed in order to add the ASK dimension to the teaching of the whole staff.

■ In addition to this, structured time for collaborative planning, team-teaching and debrief/feedback are very effective and appreciated by most staff.

■ Involve as many staff as practical/appropriate in the planning and organisation of whole-staff INSET.

■ It is important to strike the correct balance between theory and practical in-class strategies.

■ 'Live lessons' when effectively planned, observed in a guided and focused way and debriefed formally provide an excellent training tool (despite being more time-consuming to organise and more effort to manage!).

■ An appropriate guest speaker at either the beginning or end of the INSET can provide a powerful means of inspiring and motivating staff.

# Outline programme of whole-staff INSET

## INSET 1

**Suggested duration:** 2 consecutive days
**Aimed at:** All teaching staff
**Led by:** SLT, ASTs (if applicable), staff volunteers, guest speaker

### Objectives
- Provide a rationale for the introduction of a 'learning-to-learn' curriculum.
- Present the model for learning-to-learn: **A**ttitudes, **S**kills and **K**nowledge taught by all teachers alongside their own subject skills and content.
- Present and discuss the **ASK** curriculum map.
- Begin to explore strategies for teaching **ASK** through learning activities in different curriculum subject areas.

### Format
- Introductory session (whole staff): theory of ASK.
- Workshop sessions (mixed groups of staff from different subject areas) – group activities to engage with the content of the ASK curriculum.
- Observation and debrief of 'live lessons' taught by volunteer staff to invited Year 7 students.
- Plenary/close: guest speaker (Professor Guy Claxton) – 'Towards Lifelong Learners'.

### Outcomes
- All staff aware of the need for learning-to-learn and the background, national context and current thinking in this area.
- All staff introduced to the ASK curriculum map and have had the opportunity to engage with it.
- All staff have seen examples of learning-to-learn lessons being taught in different subject areas.

## INSET 2

**Suggested duration:** 1 day
**Aimed at:** All teaching staff
**Led by:** SLT, ASTs (if applicable), staff volunteers

### Objectives
- Recap learning-to-learn and the theory behind it: national context, meta-learning, Professor Guy Claxton's levels, school context, ASK curriculum map, expectation for all teachers to deliver relevant components of ASK.
- Focus in detail on certain elements of ASK; for example, memory, reflectiveness, meta-learning review.
- Develop further practical strategies for introducing ASK and learning-to-learn into Year 7 teaching.

### Format
- Introductory session (whole staff): theory of ASK.
- Four workshop sessions (mixed groups of staff from different subject areas) – group activities to engage with specific elements of the ASK curriculum (see objective 2).
- Plenary: reflection and evaluation. Staff given a pro forma on which to answer the following key questions:
  - Which **A**ttitudes, **S**kills and pieces of **K**nowledge did you learn more about today?
- What knowledge of the learning process do you feel confident to incorporate into your teaching as a result of today's training?
  - Which three action points are you prepared to commit to in order to enhance your teaching of the ASK curriculum?

➜

**157**

**Outcomes**
- All staff reminded of structure, content and expectation of delivery of the ASK curriculum.
- Staff learn strategies for building a meta-learning element into their teaching as well as learning in detail about 3 or 4 key areas of ASK.
- All staff committed to three action points to build into their Year 7 teaching at least once per fortnight.

## INSET 3

**Suggested duration:** 2 consecutive days
**Aimed at:** All teaching staff
**Led by:** SLT, curriculum leaders, guest speaker

**Objectives**
- All staff are made aware of the different areas of ASK that are required to be taught to each of Years 7, 8 and 9 and the rationale behind dividing up the curriculum in this way.
- Staff learn in detail about *progression* through the different skill areas of ASK and how to measure progression and incorporate it into their planning of effective learning-to-learn lessons.
- Staff experience progression through observing 'live' lessons and then plan to continue this progression through the specific ASK skill of 'Thinking'.

**Format**
- Introductory session (whole staff): theory of ASK. Division of curriculum between Years 7, 8 and 9 and rationale behind this.
- Curriculum leaders and second in faculty team-teach a pair of 'live' lessons demonstrating progression through the ASK skill of 'Thinking'. Other faculty members observe using prompt sheet and debrief/discuss observations.
- Structured planning time: rest of faculty plan in pairs the third lesson in the sequence on 'Thinking', extrapolating the progression still further.
- Pairs team-teach third lesson on 'Thinking' and are observed by other members of the faculty.
- Feedback and debrief: what have we learned about planning and teaching for *progression* through the ASK skills?
- Plenary/close: guest speaker (Dr Bill Lucas) – 'Learning is Learnable'.

**Outcomes**
- All staff are aware of which areas of the ASK curriculum they are expected to teach to each of Years 7, 8 and 9.
- Staff understand the need to plan for and facilitate progression through the ASK skills.
- Staff experience planning and practical strategies for teaching ASK progression.

**Figure 13.2 An outline programme of whole-school INSET on learning-to-learn and the ASK curriculum**

# 14 School leadership and learning-to-learn

'All children are artists. The problem is how to remain an artist once he grows up.'

PICASSO

## COMING UP IN THIS CHAPTER

▶ Some frequently asked questions (FAQs) and our answers to them.

While we are sure that, if you are planning to introduce learning-to-learn in your school, you will have plenty of your own ideas, we thought it would be helpful to address some of the frequently asked questions about our approach. We would like to stress that our approach is only one of many and we certainly would not wish to claim to have perfect solutions to the issues related to implementing a learning-to-learn curriculum. In fact, we see ourselves as engaged in a continuing journey and are still very much in the process of finding the answers to many, if not to all, of these questions.

1    *How do you get staff on board with the idea of learning-to-learn?*

At Villiers we started with three advanced skills teachers and an assistant headteacher who worked together with a consultant to start developing a learning-to-learn curriculum. They began with a blank sheet of paper and spent the first two months researching learning-to-learn. They put together a draft outline curriculum describing learning-to-learn Attitudes, Skills and Knowledge. In the next phase, they created a cross-curricular learning-to-learn team consisting of a small group of staff with representatives from each faculty. This team was introduced to the ideas of learning-to-learn, the content and rationale of the draft curriculum and were invited to take part in the empirical development of the curriculum through planning and testing out experimental lessons. Staff worked in pairs assisted by the advanced skills teachers with planning and reflecting on the lessons. An assistant headteacher co-ordinated the project. In addition, the teachers worked with our external consultant who visited twice in this period, which lasted six months. In that time, the team met as a group on a regular basis.

The learning-to-learn curriculum was launched with the whole staff at a two-day conference in March prior to the September start date. By the March conference, the learning-to-learn team were ready to go 'live' with their draft curriculum and, most importantly, each member of the team taught a 'live' learning-to-learn lesson to a group of students on that day. These lessons were observed by the rest of the teachers and the methodology used was discussed at the end of each lesson. Teachers were able to see how learning-to-learn could work in practice in the classroom. Each teacher was given a folder with the curriculum and with guidance on teaching learning-to-learn. The second day of the conference was used by staff to write lesson plans for learning-to-learn, assisted in each faculty by their member of the learning-to-learn team. During the 'experimental period', lesson plans were collated and stored in the school library. These were available as exemplars to help with planning. We invited a number of external visitors to the March conference and went to considerable trouble to make sure the resources were professionally presented and the catering was of a very high standard so that the whole event had a good and high-status professional feel to it.

There were a number of reasons for approaching the implementation like this:

- We wanted to have a learning-to-learn curriculum that suited our school and was owned by our staff.
- We needed a very small group of knowledgeable staff to do the initial research and thinking to devise the curriculum.
- We needed to try out ideas in the classroom to find out more and to learn about learning-to-learn.
- We were able to define and exemplify learning-to-learn in terms of classroom practice before introducing it to the whole staff.
- We had real examples that staff could use to help them write learning-to-learn lessons before they were asked to do so.
- The learning-to-learn team were representative of all subjects but small enough to form a cohesive team. The team was small enough to be taken off timetable for a number of morning or afternoon sessions.
- The experimental work of the team raised interest among many other staff, making them aware of and interested in learning-to-learn before the launch conference.
- The involvement of an external consultant, highly respected by staff, gave status to those involved in the development project.
- Implementation in the first year was with Year 7 only. This made it manageable.

**2**  *How do you ensure that staff are trained sufficiently well to deliver effective learning-to-learn lessons?*

If only teaching were like a sandwich brought from Upper Crust – always the same and very nice too! Apparently, Upper Crust achieves this by having recipes for every sandwich sold. Staff are trained to follow the recipe. It would be nice if we could give teachers recipes to follow that guaranteed quality, then the problems that Ofsted and DfES continually point out – 'the variation between departments in schools is greater than the variation between schools' – would disappear overnight.

Maybe this would be the answer: to give teachers a detailed set of learning-to-learn lesson plans and train them to teach these. We have thought about it but in our experience it does not work. People are too complex. While a 'recipe type' approach may appear to lead to consistency and may be helpful to address really poor teaching, we believe it detracts from the development of professional skills and creativity.

At Villiers, training for learning-to-learn is multilayered, overlapping and continuous, and involves a range of activities and people. It attempts to combine the raising of levels of sophistication, in quality of practice, for all staff, by introducing new staff to learning-to-learn and by coaching individual staff working at different levels in the classroom. The methods we use include:

a) *Time for collaborative planning*
   Following the first March staff conference described earlier, all departments were asked to devote their 'gained time' from Year 11 in the summer term to developing learning-to-learn lessons. The advanced skills teachers were attached to departments to support the teachers with lesson planning and evaluation so that by the end of the summer term each department had developed a bank of lessons for use in September. Providing the time for staff to plan and teach together has been essential in the development of staff expertise and confidence.

b) *Exemplar lesson plans and resources*
   We have a central electronic store of learning-to-learn lesson plans. Staff are asked to save their lesson plans in a learning-to-learn folder on the school intranet.

c) *Training days*
   In the first year of implementation of learning-to-learn, there were a further two whole-staff training days devoted to learning-to-learn and in total (in the last 18 months) there have been six training days on learning-to-learn.

d) *Teacher coaches*
   We have had a teacher coach on the staff at Villiers for the past five years and shortly after the introduction of learning-to-learn we made a new appointment to this role. Most of his coaching is on learning-to-learn. In addition, he runs workshops for teachers (attendance is voluntary) on particular aspects of the ASK curriculum.

e) *Training for specific groups of staff*
   We have given specific training for curriculum leaders focusing on role modelling the teaching of learning-to-learn.
   We have also given specific training to newly qualified teachers.

The training on learning-to-learn evolves as our expertise develops and as the curriculum grows. Our experience would suggest that it would be difficult to train staff fully in learning-to-learn in one go before they embark on teaching it. Effective training is continuous and involves a variety of approaches: coaching; whole days; small group training; time for pairs and groups of staff to develop lessons; external consultants and speakers.

**3**  *How do you motivate staff to continue teaching learning-to-learn?*

Recently, we had a temporary finance assistant working for us. When asked why she chose to take a series of temporary jobs, she explained that she had had a number of permanent jobs in the past, in large companies, but she had got bored because she had always been given one single narrowly focused job, such as writing purchase orders, to do all day, day in, day out. She explained that she liked to do different things and use all her skills. When she left us she told us how much she loved working in our school because of the variety.

Our view is that staff are motivated to continually improve by being introduced to new ideas in interesting and stimulating ways, by being encouraged to develop new ideas and new approaches to teaching, by being given time to develop new ideas with colleagues, by being assisted to make new ideas work. This gives staff the chance to develop their professional skills and professional pride. Without this, teaching can become a tedious and boring 'job'.

Expectations are important too: the expectation that teaching will continually develop and that it is never perfected. In our view, ongoing training is essential for this. Monitoring and evaluation of practice also play their part. We have found the student lesson observers are particularly helpful.

The more learning-to-learn we do, the more learning-to-learn is brought into what we do. This happens because staff understand it better through their practice and they see its relevance and how it can be extended to develop further within their subject.

It is helpful to maintain a high profile for learning-to-learn. We have a newsletter for staff, assemblies on learning-to-learn for students and learning-to-learn comes up in discussions on a regular basis.

**4**  *What made you decide to embed learning-to-learn within the traditional subject areas as opposed to teaching it as a discrete subject?*

Before deciding how to incorporate learning-to-learn we explored options for its implementation. We looked at what other schools were doing and held a staff debate about the best approach.

The options considered included:
- Teaching learning-to-learn as a discrete subject.
- Collapsing the Year 7 curriculum to teach cross-curricular projects and themes incorporating learning-to-learn.
- Embedding learning-to-learn across all subjects in the curriculum.

We chose the latter approach, even though it was more complex. Our reasons were as follows:
- When learning takes place there has to be relevant content to work with.
- Study skills teaching in PSHE did not appear to be successful. In our experience, skills learned were not applied.

- The way learning develops, according to Piaget, is from the concrete to the abstract or from the particular to the general. If we create an approach where students are practising learning skills within subjects, then looking at those learning skills objectively and if they repeat this across many subjects, it seems more likely that they will learn a generalised skill to apply in other situations. This recognises that repetition is known to be very important in learning.

- The idea of approaching learning-to-learn as a cross–curricular course based on themes/projects for Year 7 concerned us. These 'projects' would only involve a small group of teachers, who might appear to be 'an elite'. The course would become dependent on those teachers; those teachers would be taken away disproportionately from teaching other classes. In addition, we felt that students were ready to study separate subjects when they joined secondary school.

- Our aim in developing learning-to-learn is for our students to take responsibility for their own learning and this has to be across all their subjects. This has to be expected in every lesson in every subject and can only happen if that is expressed, assisted, developed and modelled by all the teachers. Learning-to-learn, for us, encompasses a change of approach as well as curriculum content and so in that sense it has to take place across the whole school.

5  *How do you know that your students are benefiting from learning-to-learn?*

We will find out the impact of learning-to-learn on our academic achievement at Villiers with the first set of KS3 SAT results for the first cohort of learning-to-learn students.

Feedback from staff and students indicates that they believe learning-to-learn is making a significant and positive impact on Villiers' students. Probably the most notable effect is the degree of initiative the students are showing now compared to before. The ethos of the school and student body has changed – students constantly make requests to organise events and appear to be more motivated, committed and knowledgeable about their learning.

6  *How do you store all of your resources and make them available to all staff?*

Learning-to-learn lesson plans and resources are stored on the school intranet and in the school library. Some classrooms also have a learning wall full of generic learning-to-learn resources.

7  *What strategies do you use to ensure the best quality planning of learning-to-learn from staff?*

We use various approaches:

a) *Exemplar lessons*

Watching lessons and creating time for staff to plan, teach and evaluate together has been very important, and a successful part of all our training days. Staff have taught live exemplar lessons on these days. The lessons are evaluated by the teachers in discussion afterwards. In addition, staff have been asked to plan in pairs during the training days and then deliver their planned lesson, as a 'live lesson', to colleagues who then evaluate it. When a lesson is actually going to be taught in front of colleagues, the planning activity has a much sharper focus than when it is a theoretical exercise. On these occasions, when the lesson must be planned and then 'delivered live', staff share their very best practice and ideas. It not only raises everybody's game, but also creates an ethos of professional focus and respect.

In addition, we give time for staff to plan together. At the start of learning-to-learn, 'gained time' in the summer term was used for planning and experimenting. More recently, staff have used 'gained time' during the Year 11 mock examinations.

b)  *Sharing lesson plans*

These are shared during meetings where staff talk through their plans, on INSET days, by delivering live lessons and by posting all lesson plans on the school intranet.

c)  *Coaching*

We have a full-time teacher coach who is an assistant headteacher and works with individual staff and groups of staff to develop their practice. He works systematically with each faculty in turn. In addition, individual staff approach him to ask for help with developing ideas.

**8**  *How do you ensure that there is no duplication or repetition of learning-to-learn skills?*

Our initial approach to learning-to-learn was to require all departments to build in all the skills into their schemes of work and to focus on particular skills for particular year groups. Repetition was not seen as an issue and, in fact, our aim was that students would be learning the same skills in different subject contexts. More recently we have considered that some skills are particularly important for some subjects and we are currently having discussions about this. It seems likely that certain subjects will have a strong focus on particular skills, although there will still be considerable overlap. For example, the PE department want to focus on 'Learning with others', but so do the science department. Maths, science, PE and history want to focus on 'Thinking skills'. English, art, design and technology, and science want to develop 'Planning'. The overlap is seen as important and duplication as a benefit.

**9**  *How have you managed to introduce student lesson observers without staff protesting?*

The introduction of student lesson observers at Villiers came at a particular point along a journey the school has been travelling for the past eight years. A few years ago it would have been very difficult to do this and the reason why it has been possible now is because the staff are used to having lesson observations and helpful feedback and they are used to the notion of continual development through professional collaboration.

Having said that, we were very careful and very deliberate about the process we used to introduce them. The key points in making it successful were:

- We saw the process in action at another school first and so we were able to talk to staff about the concrete and real experience we had had, which was very positive.
- We did not force any staff to have student lesson observers.
- We introduced the idea to staff at a full staff meeting where we presented the rationale for student lesson observers; the examples we had seen; the process we intended to follow at Villiers and emphasised how positive the experience had been for the staff we met at Matthew Moss School.
- After our visit to Matthew Moss School, and before the staff meeting, a senior member of staff deliberately worked her way around the staffroom at break times and lunchtimes talking to staff about what we had seen and how positive it had been. She asked staff if they would be interested in volunteering to have student lesson observers to see their lessons. By the time the staff meeting happened, the majority of staff were well informed about student lesson observers. In addition, prior to visiting Matthew Moss school, staff were invited to suggest questions to ask and the responses to them were discussed at a staff meeting.
- Members of the senior leadership team have been among the first staff to be observed and have feedback from the students. We believe that it is important to 'put your money where your mouth is' and to lead by example. In fact, for those senior leaders reading this and considering introducing lesson observers, the experience of being observed by students and getting their feedback is a very positive one and quite awe-inspiring: the students are so good at it!

**10** *Why bother with learning-to-learn?*

There are several reasons.

a) *To raise standards*

The achievement at Villiers is good, as measured in comparison to other similar schools, and the value added is good. However, we know we want it to be even better and to do that we have to change the way we do things so that our students can take a lot more advantage of their education. We have to help the students develop all those learning-to-learn skills and attitudes we have identified. Some students will develop good learning skills by default. These tend to be the more able students and it is almost certainly why they achieve so well; however, we cannot rely on this. We need to be explicit.

b) *To improve self-reliance*

From our analyses in the past, we know that when the students are asked to be self-reliant, apply what they know in unusual contexts or think for themselves, they flounder and often give up. The ASK curriculum is attempting to address these needs. This will help students not only to achieve good performance in exams, but also to go a lot further than this to support them in future study, work and life.

c) *To develop active minds*

We have a vision of education for our students that is much broader than the national curriculum. We would like them to leave us with lively, engaging, enquiring, and questioning minds, so that they can get the most out of life, can enjoy the new experiences they encounter, do not simply accept explanations at face value, want to play an active part in society, are interested in finding out more, can adapt as the world changes, and are aware of themselves and others and how to influence when they need to.

**11**  *How did you get the governing body on board with the idea of learning-to-learn?*

Learning-to-learn was discussed at curriculum subcommittee meetings and full governing body meetings from the time when we first started developing the curriculum. We have kept governors up to date with developments by writing about progress in reports on a regular basis.

In addition, governors have been invited to attend school training days about learning-to-learn and they have had a presentation at a full governing body meeting.

Although learning-to-learn is not within their direct school experience, the governors have been fully supportive of learning-to-learn from the start. In fact, they are very enthusiastic about the learning-to-learn curriculum, seeing its tremendous value for students. This is especially true of the parent–governors or those with school-age children who are acutely aware of their own children's learning needs.

**12**  *What have you done to inform parents about learning-to-learn and convince them that it is good for their children?*

As with governors, we have tried to keep parents informed from the start by:
- Informing parents about learning-to-learn at meetings and parents' evenings.
- Showing demonstration lessons at open evenings.
- Writing about learning-to-learn in our school magazine and school newsletter.

The response has been positive.

Currently, we are debating whether to have a learning-to-learn report. In addition, we are piloting student self-assessment of learning-to-learn. Our next edition of the student planner will include details of the learning-to-learn curriculum, a self-assessment grid and a parent-student assessment grid.

**13**  *How will you convince Ofsted inspectors that learning-to-learn is worthwhile?*

The new Ofsted framework appears to place a strong emphasis on learning, student progress and the student voice. In principle, we imagine that the learning-to-learn curriculum will be welcomed. The DfES appear to be placing considerable emphasis on learning-to-learn and it is included within the Learning Gateways of the Specialist Schools and Academies Trust.

We are conscious that we must be able to demonstrate that our learning-to-learn curriculum does 'what it says on the packet'. That it does help the students that attend Villiers to become better learners.

We can show Ofsted what we have done and how we have done it. They can observe learning-to-learn in action. However, we know that we must be able to demonstrate that the ASK curriculum has had a positive impact on the students and the school. To this end, we have collected data from students and staff about their perceptions of learning-to-learn and its effects. In addition, we are building an assessment of learning-to-learn into our assessment cycle so that we have student learning-to-learn achievement data alongside subject-specific achievement data. As the ASK cohorts come through, we will have data on their overall performance in SATs and GCSEs as well as question-level data to show trends and changes in student learning.

**14** *What role do teaching assistants and other non-teaching staff have in supporting the learning-to-learn curriculum?*

As with most secondary schools, the number of non-teaching staff at Villiers is growing. We try to involve the non-teachers in as much of the curriculum, teaching and learning and leadership development as we can. In recent years, we have come a long way. Now it is quite usual for non-teachers to come forward to sit on working parties and to organise extracurricular clubs and events.

Teaching assistants are in the classroom every day and they are clearly directly involved in this aspect of the school. Technicians, the network manager, external links co-ordinator and learning resources centre manager are also very involved in lessons and in the curriculum.

About four years ago, we undertook some extensive training with the teaching assistants covering: how to facilitate learning, different learning styles, how to make learning material accessible, what to do to differentiate learning and how to plan effectively alongside teachers. This training also instigated a shift in focus for the teaching assistants – away from supporting one or two individual students in a classroom, towards working with the teacher to support the class and individuals within the class. When we introduced learning-to-learn, the teaching assistants were well placed to take it up with the teachers and the students.

We made it compulsory for all non-teaching support staff to attend our first whole-staff learning-to-learn conference, so that they would be introduced to the ASK curriculum. Since then, other learning-to-learn training days have been attended by all our teaching assistants and most of our senior technicians, our learning resources centre manager and our external links co-ordinator. This has meant that the non-teaching staff are familiar with the language, ideas and techniques used in teaching learning-to-learn, so they are able to work with teachers to support it.

The learning resources centre manager has bought many resources for teachers and students; she helps teachers prepare and she works directly with students, both formally and informally. The technicians get involved in learning-to-learn lessons; the ICT network and resources are extensive and support student learning and communication; the network manager works with students on preparing videos and websites to support personalised learning. The external links co-ordinator works directly with teams of students to organise conferences and other student-led events. Examples of this work with DVD coverage are available via our website (www.villiers.ealing.sch.uk).

My experience is that the non-teaching staff are enthusiastic about 'getting stuck in' and if given the information they need, the opportunities and encouragement, they will do so.

## Conclusion

We believe learning-to-learn is an essential and central part of our students' experience as learners at school, not only because of the impact that it has on achievement, but also because of the positive effects on students' disposition towards learning, life and abilities to deal with life's events.

The response from Harold Macmillan when asked what a prime minister most feared was, 'Events, dear boy, events.' We believe that a good education equips people to be able to deal with 'events' as best as possible.

# 15 Creating lifelong learners

*'If we value independence, if we are disturbed by the growing conformity of knowledge, of values, of attitudes, which our present system induces, then we may wish to set up conditions of learning which make for uniqueness, for self-direction, and for self-initiated learning.'*

CARL ROGERS

## COMING UP IN THIS CHAPTER

▶ A look at the place and significance of learning–to–learn in schools of the future.

What is education for? What are schools for? These are enormous questions that are often left unanswered or taken for granted. And although philosophers have debated these questions for centuries, societies often accept what already exists without too much questioning. And how often do we, as teachers and professionals at the very centre of learning, stop to think about the purpose of education and the role of schools within that purpose?

Different people have distinct ideas as illustrated by the following quotations.

'Theories and goals of education don't matter a whit if you don't consider your students to be human beings.'

*Lou Ann Walker*

'Education is for improving the lives of others and for leaving your community and world better than you found it.'

*Marian Wright Edelman*

'The illiterate of the twenty-first century will not be those who cannot read and write, but those who cannot learn, unlearn, and relearn.'

*Alvin Toffler*

Perhaps one of the most valuable aims of education is to leave young people with a love of learning so that they want to continue when they are no longer obliged to do so by law. Explicitly, teaching the skills of learning in such a way that students become good, confident and successful learners serves a dual purpose. It maximises the progress they make at school but also equips and inspires them to continue their learning above and beyond school and throughout life.

Our experience shows that students who have been exposed to learning-to-learn begin to develop the skills to help themselves, they understand learning and are more motivated and determined to succeed. So, it is justified even against the narrow objective of improving exam performance. But we also know that most teachers have a much broader vision and passion for education than this. This is most easily seen when teachers talk about their aspirations for the future of the young people they meet and work with in their schools. This is where learning-to-learn is at its most powerful. Imagine the lifelong potential of any learner who has the ability to respond confidently to challenging and unfamiliar situations, can think effectively and creatively, can plan and solve problems, and can make a positive impact on other people's lives. In our view, these are the life skills that we all need, and we often hear said that it is what society needs for its citizens of tomorrow.

The more we develop learning-to-learn at Villiers, the more amazed we are with the capabilities of our students and of their readiness to embrace a learning partnership with their teachers. This has been most obvious with the student lesson observers. Their maturity, ability and willingness has not ceased to impress us and others outside our school. This has started to raise questions about whether we, in our school and the system itself, underestimate students, whether we dumb down our students' natural capacity to excel as learners.

John Abbot in his book *The Unfinished Revolution* (2000) suggests that our system, as it is organised now, does not recognise the biological imperative of adolescence – that is, to break away from the parent and find independence. He suggests that our school system from the outset should be geared towards helping young people acquire the capabilities to be independent and that by the time young people reach 14, we should be ready to give them responsibility and choice and encourage them to step into adulthood. He argues that responsible, capable, skilled young people would be able to do this if given the right foundations.

> 'At all levels of the education system it seems as if the system is simply reluctant to let go of students. It is as if no learning is taking place unless the students are being taught. Rather than weaning youngsters, the system seems bent on playing down their ability to do something for themselves. In a variety of subtle and not so subtle ways, Western society has trivialised all levels of young people in school. Is it any wonder teenagers say they feel bored, uninvolved and often in conflict with a world that tells them what to do rather than expects them to work it out for themselves.'

## Schools of the future

As we have developed learning-to-learn we have increasingly thought about the implications of this for our school and even for the system we work within. When students have an awareness and understanding of their own learning, this inevitably brings the whole field of personalised learning to the fore. Choice and flexibility in learning are issues that cannot be avoided. Once students are capable learners, they will not be kept happy with learning activities that do not meet their needs and interests. Even without an explicit learning-to-learn curriculum in place, young people are exposed to such choice within their environment that schools cannot avoid these issues. We only have to consider for a moment what is available through electronic media (computers, mobile phones, TV, ipods and so on) and what is the norm for young people in our secondary schools today, to recognise that schools have to change otherwise they will lose their audience, at least intellectually and emotionally, if not physically.

## Flexible schools

Is it possible that in the future we could have schools where young people do not necessarily attend between 8.30 a.m. and 3.30 p.m. and that they spend some of their time learning independently? Rather like the flexible workforce pioneered by some businesses, students would come to school for those parts of their learning that need to take place with others. These experiences would be specially targeted for particular learning objectives and might involve others who are not teachers; for example, artists, business people, skilled artisans. In those cases, they might learn in groups that are bigger or smaller than traditional class sizes. We would need a good virtual school to support this, using the very best of what is known about virtual learning and supported by contact with dedicated teachers, and students would need excellent learning attitudes and skills. Perhaps this would be possible for 14–19-year-olds, after they have developed these at Key Stage 1, 2 and 3.

Ultimately, we would like to see a change to our system so that teachers and schools can genuinely help each individual to learn as effectively as they can and to help all young people retain their natural enthusiasm for learning, not only by going with the 'grain of the brain' as John Abbot says, but also by adapting to the changes in our world.

We hope that there will be real system changes that will facilitate the development of real personalised learning so that we can take these ideas to the next level and recognise our students' powers to learn in many different and creative ways. We would like our students to be able to make significant and real choices about how and what to learn so that as a result of this, young people leave our system with a better standard of education and as genuine lifelong learners.

For this to be a possibility, our education system would need to start developing learning-to-learn from an early age, so that by the time young people join our secondary schools they would have good learning skills and, most importantly, would have developed the attitudes of learning discussed in this book. Essentially, we would be asking our students to take a much more mature approach to their learning.

Over the centuries, philosophers have emphasised the primacy of learning over knowledge; yet our system is still dominated by the transmission of knowledge. We hope this will change and we have tried, through our work on learning-to-learn at Villiers High School, to reverse the trend. By sharing our experience, we hope that, in a small way, we may help and inspire you to continue exploring the same path.

# Useful resources

Abbot, John and Ryan, Terry (2000) *The Unfinished Revolution*, Network Educational Press

Allan, Dave, Kingdon, Matt, Murrin, Kris and Rudkin, Daz (2002) *What if! Sticky Wisdom: How to Start a Creative Revolution at Work*, Capstone

Anderson, Lorin W. and Sosniak, Lauren A. (1994) *Bloom's Taxonomy of Educational Objectives: a Forty-year Retrospective*, University of Chicago Press

BBC Worldwide (2004) *A Child of Our Time 2004. 3. The Making of Me*

Berger, John (1972) *Ways of Seeing*, Pelican

Berman, Michael and Brown, David (2000) *The Power of the Metaphor*, Crown House Publishing

Bransford, John D., Brown, Ann L. and Cocking, Rodney R. (2000) *How People Learn: Brain, Mind, Experience and School*, National Academy Press

Burnett, Gary (2002) *Learning to Learn,* Crown House Publishing

Cavigioli, Oliver and Harris, Ian (2004) *Reaching Out to All Thinkers*, Network Educational Press

Cavigllioli, Oliver, Harris, Ian and Tindall, Bill (2002) *Thinking Skills & Eye Q*, Network Educational Press

Clarke, Darren (2005) *Golf – The Mind Factor*, Hodder and Stoughton

Claxton, Guy (1998) *Hare Brain, Tortoise Mind*, Fourth Estate

Claxton, Guy (2003) *Building Learning Power*, TLO

Covey, Stephen R. (1989) *The Seven Habits of Highly Successful People*, Simon and Schuster

De Bono, Edward (1970) *Lateral Thinking*, Harper and Row

De Bono, Edward (1993) *Teach Your Child To Think*, Penguin

Foster, Jack (2001) *Ideaship: How to get Ideas Flowing in Your Workplace*, Berrett-Koehler

Gallwey, W. Timothy (1974) *The Inner Game of Tennis*, Pan

Gardner, Howard (1993) *Multiple Intelligences: the Theory in Practice*, Basic Books

Ginnis, Paul (2002) *The Teachers' Toolkit*, Crown House Publishing

Greany, Toby and Rodd, Jill (2003) *Creating a Learning to Learn School*, Campaign for Learning

Greeff, Annie (2005) *Resilience*, Vol. 1, Crown House Publishing

Gregorc, Anthony F. (1985) *Inside Styles: Beyond the Basics*, Gregorc Associates

Gregorc, Anthony F. (1998) *The Mind Styles Model; Theory; Principles and Practice*, Gregorc Associates

Gregory, R.L. (1997) *Eye and Brain: the Psychology of Seeing*, Oxford University Press

Janni, Nicholas and Olivier, Richard (2004) *Peak Performance Presentations*, Spiro Press

Laing, R.D. (1970) *Knots*, Penguin

Levi, Primo (1998) *The Drowned and the Saved*, Michael Joseph

Lipman Matthew (2003) *Thinking in Education*, 2nd edn, Cambridge University Press

Lucas, Bill (2001) *Power up your Mind: Learn Faster, Work Smarter*, Nicholas Brealey

Lucas, Bill (2005) *Discover Your Hidden Talents*, Network Educational Press

Lucas, Bill and Greany, Toby (2000) *Schools in the Learning Age*, Campaign for Learning

Lucas, Bill, Greany, Toby, Rodd, Jill and Wicks, Ray (2002) *Teaching Students How To Learn: Research, Practice and INSET Resources*, Campaign for Learning

Miller, George A. (1956) 'The magical number seven, plus or minus two: some limits on our capacity for processing information', *The Psychological Review*, 63, 81–97

Persaud, Raj (2005) *The Motivated Mind*, Bantam Press

Rockett, Mel and Percival, Simon (2002) *Thinking for Learning*, Network Educational Press

Rose, Steven (1993) *The Making of Memory: From Molecules to Mind*, Bantam Books

Smith, Alistair (2002) *The Brain's Behind It*, Network Educational Press

Strang, Juliet, Daniels, Sandra and Bell, John (1991) *Assessment Matters No. 6: Planning and Carrying Out Investigations*, School Examination and Assessment Council

Webb Young, James (2003) *A Technique for Producing Ideas*, McGraw Hill

# Index